ECONOMIC AND SOCIAL COMMISSION
FOR WESTERN ASIA

اللجنة الاقتصادية والاجتماعية
لغربي آسيا

نشرة السكان والإحصاءات الحيوية في منطقة الإسكوا

BULLETIN ON POPULATION AND VITAL STATISTICS IN THE ESCWA REGION

Tenth Issue   العدد العاشر

الأمم المتحدة
نيويورك، ٢٠٠٧

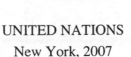

UNITED NATIONS
New York, 2007

United Nations Publication
E/ESCWA/SCU/2007/7
ISBN. 978-92-1-128316-7
ISSN. 1020-7368
Sales No. E/A.08.II.L.3
07-0493

Contents

المحتويات

List of Figures

قائمة بالأشكال البيانية

شكل	الهرم السكاني للبحرين، تعداد 2001	1
شكل	الهرم السكاني لمصر تعداد 2004	2
شكل	الهرم السكاني لمصر تعداد 1997	3
شكل	الهرم السكاني للاردن تعداد 2004	4
شكل	الهرم السكاني للكويت تعداد 2005	5
شكل	الهرم السكاني لعمان تعداد 2003	6
شكل	الهرم السكاني لفلسطين تعداد 1997	7
شكل	الهرم السكاني لقطر تعداد 2004	8
شكل	الهرم السكاني للسعودية تعداد 2004	9
شكل	الهرم السكاني لسورية تعداد 2004	10
شكل	الهرم السكاني للامارات تعداد 2005	11
شكل	الهرم السكاني لليمن تعداد 2004	12
شكل	معدل وفيات الرضع في بعض بلدان الاسكوا في عام 2000 و 2005	13
شكل	معدل الخصوبة الكلية لكل امرأة في البحرين	14
شكل	معدل الخصوبة الكلية لكل امرأة في مصر	15
شكل	معدل الخصوبة الكلية لكل امرأة في العراق	16
شكل	معدل الخصوبة الكلية لكل امرأة في الكويت	17
شكل	معدل الخصوبة الكلية لكل امرأة في قطر	18
شكل	معدل الخصوبة الكلية لكل امرأة في الامارات العربية المتحدة	19

Introduction

The Economic and Social Commission for Western Asia (ESCWA) is pleased to present the Tenth issue of the Bulletin on Population and Vital Statistics in the ESCWA Region.

The purpose of the publication is to provide available data and statistics on ESCWA countries' registered vital events (births, deaths, marriage and divorce), as well as the main indicators for each of these events and to compare them with the estimates prepared by the United Nations Population Division[1] in New York.

This issue includes vital statistics and indicators from 2000 to the date of preparation of this publication. Data before 2000 are available in the previous issues of the bulletin. The Bulletin has been revised where some changes have been introduced and reflected under each of its three sections.

The first section covers the population in ESCWA region; the second section presents data on the fertility and mortality; and the third section provides statistics and indicators related to marriage and divorce.

In order to standardize the basis of comparison, the estimates of the United Nations Population Division (2000, 2002, 2004 and 2006 Revisions) were used as the denominator for vital events in the calculation of the rates.

Data contained in this Bulletin were compiled from national statistical sources including: annual statistical yearbooks and vital statistics publications and by using questionnaires prepared by ESCWA for this issue. Data for Lebanon were obtained from the Ministry of Interior.

We hope that this publication will meet the needs of data users, especially researchers, academics and those working in the field of population, reproductive health and development by providing a comprehensive picture on population growth and its dynamics.

Last but not least, the Executive Secretary would like to thank the member states for providing her with the requested data and hope for maintaining this fruitful cooperation.

[1] United Nations, Department of Economic and Social Affairs. *World Population Prospects. The 2000 Revision. Vol.. 1: Comprehensive Tables.* New York, 2001, and *World Population Prospects. The 2002 Revision. Vol.. 1: Comprehensive Tables.* New York, 2003, and *World Population Prospects. The 2004 Revision. Vol. 1: Comprehensive Tables.* New York, 2005, and *World Population Prospects. The 2006 Revision. Vol. 1: Comprehensive Tables.* New York, 2007.

مقدمة

يسر اللجنة الاقتصادية والاجتماعية لغربي آسيا (الإسكوا) أن تقدم العدد العاشر من "نشرة السكان والإحصاءات الحيوية في منطقة الإسكوا".

وتهدف النشرة إلى عرض البيانات والإحصاءات المتوفرة عن الوقائع الحيوية المسجلة في البلدان الأعضاء في الإسكوا (المواليد، الوفيات، الزواج، والطلاق)، وعرض بعض المؤشرات الرئيسية المشتملة بكل من هذه الوقائع مقارنة ببعض التقديرات التي أعدتها شعبة السكان في الأمم المتحدة في نيويورك.[1]

وقد تضمّن هذا العدد إحصاءات ومؤشرات منذ العام 2000 وحتى تاريخ إعداد هذه النشرة. بيانات ما قبل عام 2000 متوفرة في الأعداد السابقة للنشرة. وقد تمت مراجعة النشرة وإدخال بعض التعديلات عليها مشار إليها تحت كل من أجزائها الثلاثة.

يغطي القسم الأول بيانات عن السكان في المنطقة؛ ثم يعرض القسم الثاني إحصاءات الخصوبة والوفيات في حين يقدم القسم الثالث الإحصاءات والمؤشرات الخاصة بالزواج والطلاق.

وتوخياً لتوحيد أساس المقارنة، استخدمت تقديرات شعبة السكان في الأمم المتحدة في نيويورك (مراجعة العام 2000، و2002، و2004، و2006) بصفتها مقاسماً للوقائع الحيوية في احتساب المعدلات.

هذا واستخدمت البيانات المستخدمة في هذه النشرة من المصادر الإحصائية الوطنية مثل المجموعات الإحصائية السنوية ونشرات الإحصاءات الحيوية ومن استبيانات أعدتها الإسكوا لهذا الغرض. استخدمت بيانات لبنان من وزارة الداخلية.

ونأمل أن تلبي هذه النشرة احتياجات مستخدمي البيانات، ولاسيما الباحثين والأكاديميين والعاملين في مجال السكان والصحة الإنجابية والتنمية من خلال إعطاء صورة شاملة عن نمو السكان وديناميكيته.

وأخيراً وليس أخيراً تود الأمانة التنفيذية للإسكوا تقديم الشكر إلى الدول الأعضاء على تزويدها بالبيانات المطلوبة وتأمل الاستمرار بهذا التعاون المثمر.

[1] الأمم المتحدة، إدارة الشؤون الاقتصادية والاجتماعية، آفاق سكان العالم، مراجعة عام 2000، الجزء الأول: الجداول الشاملة، نيويورك 2001، وآفاق سكان العالم، مراجعة عام 2002، الجزء الأول: الجداول الشاملة، نيويورك 2003، وآفاق سكان العالم، مراجعة عام 2004، الجزء الأول: الجداول الشاملة، نيويورك 2005، وآفاق سكان العالم، مراجعة عام 2006، الجزء الأول: الجداول الشاملة، نيويورك 2007.

DEFINITIONS[1]:

The following vital events included in the Bulletin are:

1. Live birth

2. Death

3. Marriage

4. Divorce

They are defined as follows:

1. Live birth occurrence

Live birth is the complete expulsion or extraction from its mother of a product of conception, irrespective of the duration of pregnancy, which, after such separation, breathes or shows any other evidence of life such as beating of the heart, pulsation of the umbilical cord, or definite movement of voluntary muscles, whether or not the umbilical cord has been cut or the placenta is attached; each product of such a birth is considered livebirths.

2. Death occurrence

Death is the permanent disappearance of all evidence of life at any time after live birth has taken place (post-natal cessation of vital functions without capability of resuscitation). This definition therefore excludes foetal death.

3. Marriage occurrence

Marriage is the act, ceremony or process by which the legal relationship of husband and wife is constituted. The legality of the union may be established by civil, religious or other means as recognized by the laws of each country.

[1] Source: United Nations, "Demographic Yearbook 1995"

تعريفات[1]:

الوقائع الحيوية التي احتوت عليها هذه النشرة هي:

١- الولادة الحية

٢- الوفاة

٣- الزواج

٤- الطلاق

وتعريفاتها كما يلي:

١- واقعة الولادة الحية

الولادة الحية هي الخروج الكامل أو الانفصال الكامل لناتج الحمل من جسم أمه أو يبدو بصرف النظر عن مدة الحمل، التي يكون، بعد الانفصال على هذا النحو، تنفس عليه أي دليل آخر على الحياة مثل ضربات القلب أو نبض الحبل السري، أو حركة مؤكدة عن العضلات الإرادية، سواء أكان الحبل السري قد قطع أم لم يقطع أو كانت المشيمة متصلة به أم غير متصلة؛ ويعتبر كل ناتج للولادة على هذا النحو مولودا حيا.

٢- واقعة الوفاة

الوفاة هي الزوال الدائم لجميع الأدلة على الحياة بشكل دائم في أي وقت بعد حدوث الولادة (توقف الوظائف الحيوية بعد الولادة مع انعدام إمكانية الإنعاش). ومن ثم فإن هذا التعريف لا يشمل الوفاة الجنينية.

٣- واقعة الزواج

الزواج هو الفعل أو الإعلان أو العملية التي تنشئ العلاقة القانونية بين الزوج والزوجة. ويمكن اكتساب هذا الإعلان الصفة القانونية بأجراء مدني أو ديني أو بأي أجراء آخر يتفق مع قوانين البلد.

[1] المصدر: "الكتاب الديموغرافي ١٩٩٥" للأمم المتحدة

4. Divorce occurrence

Divorce is a final dissolution of a marriage, that is, the separation of husband and wife which confers on the parties the right to remarriage under civil, religious and/or other provisions, according to the laws of each country.

VITAL RATES[2]

The vital rates contained in this publication are the following:

I. Births and Fertility Rates:

1. Crude Birth Rate (CBR)
2. General Fertility Rate (GFR)
3. Age Specific Fertility Rate (ASFR)
4. Total Fertility Rate (TFR)
5. Gross Reproduction Rate (GRR)
6. Mean Age of Childbearing (MACB)

II. Mortality Rates:

7. Crude Death Rate (CDR)
8. Infant Mortality Rate (IMR)
9. Crude Death Rate by Cause

III. Marriage Rates:

10. Crude Marriage Rate (CMR)
11. Mean Age at First Marriage

[2] Source: United Nations, World Population Prospects: the 1996 Revision

---

4- وقعة الطلاق

الطلاق هو فسخ نهائي لرابطة الزواج أي التفريق بين الزوج والزوجة بشكل يعطي كلا من الطرفين الحق في الزواج من جديد طبقا للأحكام المدنية و/أو الدينية و/أو غيرها، وفقا لقوانين كل بلد بعينه.

المعدلات الحيوية[2]

ويحوي هذا العدد المعدلات الحيوية التالية:

I. معدلات المواليد والخصوبة

1- معدل المواليد الخام
2- معدل الخصوبة العام
3- معدل الخصوبة العمرية
4- معدل الخصوبة الكلية
5- معدل الإحلال الإجمالي
6- متوسط عمر المرأة عند الإنجاب

II. معدلات الوفيات

7- معدل الوفيات الخام
8- معدل وفيات الرضع
9- معدل وفيات الخام حسب السبب

III. معدلات الزواج

10- معدل الزواج الخام
11- متوسط العمر عند الزواج الأول

[2] المصدر: الأمم المتحدة، آفاق سكان العالم: مراجعة سنة 1996.

IV. معدلات الطلاق:

12- معدل الطلاق الخام

وطريقة حساب المعدلات الحيوية كما يلي:

المنهجية

I. معدلات المواليد والخصوبة

1- معدل المواليد الخام

وهو عدد المواليد أحياء خلال سنة معينة لكل ألف من السكان في منتصف السنة:

$$CBR = \frac{B}{P} \times 1000$$

حيث:

B: عدد الولادات الحية التي حدثت خلال سنة معينة (أو المتوسط السنوي لفترة زمنية).

P: تقدير السكان في منتصف السنة (أو منتصف الفترة الزمنية).

2- معدل الخصوبة العام

وهو عدد المواليد أحياء لكل ألف امرأة في سن الإنجاب (15-49) في منتصف السنة

$$GFR = \frac{B}{F_{15-49}} \times 1000$$

حيث:

B: عدد الولادات الحية التي حدثت خلال سنة معينة (أو المتوسط السنوي لفترة زمنية).

IV. Divorce Rates:

12. Crude Divorce Rate

The vital rates formulas are as follows:

METHODOLGY

I. Births and Fertility Rates:

1. Crude birth rate (CBR)

The number of live births during a particular calendar year per 1000 mid-year total population:

$$CBR = \frac{B}{P} \times 1000$$

Where:

B: number of live births that occurred during a particular calendar year (or average annual births of a period).

P: mid-year (or mid-interval) population for the same year or period.

2. General Fertility Rate

The number of live births per 1000 mid-year female population of childbearing age (15-49)

$$GFR = \frac{B}{F_{15-49}} \times 1000$$

Where:

B: number of live births that occurred during a particular calendar year (or average of a period).

F_{15-49}: mid-year female population aged (15-49) (i.e. in childbearing age).

3. Age Specific Fertility Rate (ASFR)

The annual number of live births per 1000 women of a specified age. Expressed symbolically, it is defined as:

$$_nf_x = \frac{_nB_x}{_nF_x} \times 1000$$

Where:

$_nf_x$: is age-specific fertility rate of women aged x to x+n years.

$_nF_x$: is the number of women aged x to x+n years at mid-year.

$_nB_x$: is the number of births to women aged x to x+n years during a calendar year or annual average for an interval.

n: is the number of years in the age interval.

4. Total Fertility Rate (TFR)

It is obtained by summing the age-specific fertility rates for single years of age over the childbearing span and it is computed on a "per woman" basis. It states the total number of children an average woman would bear during her lifetime if she were to bear children throughout her reproductive years at rates specified by the schedule of age-specific fertility rate for the particular year or time interval. It assumes that this hypothetical woman does not die before the end of her childbearing age (i.e. age 50).

The TFR formula is:

$$TFR = n \sum_{15}^{49} \left(\frac{_nB_x}{_nF_x} \right)$$

F_{15-49}: تقدير النساء في سن الحمل (أو منتصف السنة) في الفترة (15-49).

3- معدل الخصوبة العمرية

و هو عدد الولادات الحية سنويا لكل ألف امرأة في عمر معين، ويعبر عنها في الصيغة التالية:

$$_nf_x = \frac{_nB_x}{_nF_x} \times 1000$$

حيث:

$_nf_x$: هو معدل الخصوبة العمرية للنساء في العمر x الى x+n

$_nF_x$: هو عدد النساء في الفئة العمرية x الى x+n في منتصف السنة.

$_nB_x$: عدد المواليد للنساء في الفئة العمرية x الى x+n أو المتوسط السنوي لفترة زمنية معينة.

n: طول الفئة العمرية.

4- معدل الخصوبة الكلية

وتجمع الحصول عليه بتجميع معدلات الخصوبة العمرية للسنوات الفردية خلال مدى سن الحمل، وهي تحسب لكل امرأة. وهي تعطي إجمالي عدد الأطفال الذين في المتوسط تنجبهم السيدة طول حياتها على أساس أن إنجابها يحدث خلال معدلات الخصوبة العمرية السائدة خلال السنة المعينة. وهو يفترض أن المرأة سوف تنقل على قيد الحياة حتى نهاية تقريبا لفترة الإنجابية.

والمعدل كما يلي:

حيث المعدل يحسب عادة من بيانات مبوبة في فئات عمرية ن (وعادة ما تكون فئات خمسية).

5- معدل الإحلال الإجمالي (GRR)

وهو مناظر تماماً لمعدل الخصوبة الكلية (TFR)، إلا أنه يعود إلى المواليد الإناث فقط. وهذا المقياس يبين عن كم من الأطفال الإناث اللاتي تنجبهم الأم خلال فترة حياتها الإنجابية، إذا تعرضت لمعدلات الخصوبة العمرية لإنجاب الإناث، والتي سجلت خلال سنة معينة (أو لمتوسط سنوي لفترة زمنية معينة)، أو بمعنى آخر أنها تقوم على أساس معدلات الخصوبة العمرية للمواليد الإناث فقط.

وإذا ضربنا معدل الخصوبة الكلية (TFR) في نسبة إجمالي المواليد الإناث إلى إجمالي المواليد خلال السنة، سوف نحصل على تقدير قريب جداً لمعدل الإحلال الإجمالي (GRR).

6- متوسط عمر المرأة عند الإنجاب

وهذا يتم الحصول عليه بضرب النسبة المئوية لجملة المواليد التي أنجبت لكل فئة عمرية للأمهات، بضربها في مركز الفئة العمرية، وبالتجميع على مدى الفئات العمرية.

II. معدلات الوفيات:

7- معدل الوفيات الخام

وهو عدد الوفيات خلال سنة معينة ومكان معين لكل ألف من السكان في منتصف السنة. ويحسب كالآتي:

$$CDR = \frac{D}{P} \times 1000$$

حيث:

D: هو إجمالي عدد الوفيات في منطقة معينة خلال سنة معينة (أو المتوسط السنوي لفترة زمنية معينة).

P: هو تقدير عدد السكان في منتصف السنة (أو الفترة الزمنية) للمقيمين في تلك المنطقة خلال هذه السنة (أو الفترة الزمنية).

Where data are grouped into age intervals of n (usually 5) years.

5. Gross Reproduction Rate (GRR)

It is identical to TFR except that it refers to female births only. This measure indicates how many daughters a woman would bear during her lifetime if, throughout her reproductive life, she is exposed to the age-specific rate of bearing female infant that is recorded for a particular year or certain interval of time. In other words, it is based on ASFR for female births only.

If we multiply the TFR by the proportion of all births in the year that were female, we will obtain a very close approximation of the GRR.

6. Mean Age of Childbearing (MACB)

This is obtained by multiplying the percentage of total births that occur in each age interval by the mid-point of that age interval, then summing across all intervals and dividing the resulting total by 100.

II. Mortality rates:

7. Crude Death Rate (CDR)

The crude death rate is the number of deaths at a certain area during a calendar year per 1000 of mid-year population. It is calculated as:

$$CDR = \frac{D}{P} \times 1000$$

Where:

D: is the total number of deaths at a certain area during a calendar year (or annual average of an interval period).

P: is the mid-year (or mid-period) population living in that area during that year (or period).

8. Infant Mortality Rate (IMR)

Infant mortality rate is the number of infant deaths (excluding foetal deaths) per 1000 livebirths. It is calculated as::

$$IMR = \frac{D_0^t}{B^t} \times 1000$$

Where:

D_0^t: is the number of infant deaths (excluding foetal deaths) between birth and before reaching the 1st birthday, among residents in an area during calendar year t (or annual average infant deaths for an interval period).

B^t: is the total number of births within the same year t (or interval period).

9. Crude Death Rate by Cause:

The number of deaths from a given cause or group of causes of death at a certain area during a calendar year (or annual average death for an interval period) per 100,000 of the mid-year population. It is calculated as:

$$= \frac{D_c}{P} \times 100,000$$

Where:

D_c: represents deaths from a particular cause or group of causes of death.

P: the population exposed to risk of death from particular cause or group of causes.

8- معدل وفيات الرضيع:

وهو عدد وفيات الرضع (لا تشمل وفيات الأجنة لكل 1000 مولود حي) ويحسب بالصيغة التالية:

$$IMR = \frac{D_0^t}{B^t} \times 1000$$

حيث:

D_0^t: عدد وفيات الرضع (لا تشمل وفيات الأجنة) أي أقل من سنة وذلك فيما بين المقيمين في منطقة معينة خلال سنة معينة t (أو المتوسط السنوي لوفيات الرضيع خلال فترة زمنية معينة).

B^t: إجمالي عدد المواليد أحياء خلال نفس السنة (أو الفترة الزمنية المعينة).

9- معدلات الوفيات الخام حسب السبب:

وهو عدد الوفيات التي تحدث عن سبب معين أو مجموعة معينة من أسباب الوفاة في منطقة معينة وخلال سنة معينة (أو المتوسط السنوي لفترة زمنية معينة) لكل مائة ألف من السكان في منتصف السنة (أو متوسط الفترة الزمنية) ويحسب كما يلي:

$$= \frac{D_c}{P} \times 100,000$$

حيث:

D_c: تعبر عن الوفيات الناتجة عن سبب معين أو مجموعة معينة من أسباب الوفاة.

P: عدد السكان المعرضين لخطر الوفاة من هذا السبب أو المجموعة من أسباب الوفاة.

III. Marriage and Divorce Rates:

10. Crude Marriage Rate (CMR)

Crude marriage rate is the ratio of the marriages during the year in an area to the average population in that year. The value is expressed in 1000 inhabitants and it is calculated as:

$$CMR = \frac{M}{P} \times 1000$$

Where:

M: is the total number of marriages occurred at a certain area during a calendar year (or annual average of an interval period).

P: is the total number of person years lived by the population, counted as the mid-year population (or mid interval population).

11. The Mean Age at First Marriage:

The mean age of women (or men) when they first get married. For a given calendar year, the mean age of women (or men) at first marriage can be calculated using the first marriage rates by age. Calculated in this way, the mean age is not weighted, i.e. the different numbers of women (or men) at each age are not taken into account.

III. معدلات الزواج و الطلاق:

10- معدل الزواج الخام

معدل الزواج الخام هو نسبة الزيجات في سنة معينة ومنطقة معينة لكل ألف من السكان، ويحسب كما يلي:

حيث:

M: هو إجمالي عدد الزيجات التي تمت في منطقة معينة خلال سنة معينة (أو المتوسط السنوي لفترة زمنية معينة).

P: إجمالي عدد السنوات التي عاشها الأفراد خلال السنة وتحسب بعدد السكان في منتصف السنة (أو منتصف الفترة الزمنية).

11- متوسط العمر عند الزواج الأول:

متوسط العمر للنساء (أو للرجال) عند الزواج الأول، ويمكن احتساب متوسط العمر، وطريقة الحساب هذا لا يكون متوسط العمر موزوناً أي لا يؤخذ بعين الاعتبار عدد النساء (أو الرجال) حسب العمر.

12. Crude Divorce Rate

Crude divorce rate is the ratio of the number of divorces during the year to the average population in that year. The value is expressed in 1000 inhabitants. It is calculated as::

$$= \frac{Div}{P} \ X \ 1000$$

Where:

Div: is the total number of divorces occurred at a certain area during a calendar year (or annual average of an interval period).

P: is the total number of person years lived by the population living at the same area during the same calendar year (or the interval period), given by the mid-year (or mid-period) population.

Data not available

Negligible or zero

12- معدل طلاق الخام

ومعدل الطلاق الخام هو نسبة عدد حالات الطلاق في سنة معينة ومنطقة معينة لكل ألف من السكان، ويحسب كما يلي:

حيث:

Div: هو إجمالي عدد واقعات الطلاق التي حدثت في منطقة معينة خلال سنة معينة (أو المتوسط السنوي لفترة زمنية معينة).

P: إجمالي عدد السنوات التي عاشها الأفراد الذين يقيمون في منطقة معينة وخلال نفس السنة (أو خلال الفترة الزمنية) ويمثله السكان في منتصف السنة (أو منتصف الفترة الزمنية).

بيانات غير متوفرة

ضئيل أو صفر

القسم الأول
Section One

السكان
Population

Section I of this Bulletin, entitled "Population", presents data on population size in the ESCWA region. It contains 13 tables and 12 population pyramids for ESCWA member countries.

(a) In this issue, twelve country tables were added on population distribution by age groups, nationality and sex, in accordance with the latest census data of member countries. All ESCWA member countries, with the exception of Lebanon, conduct a population census every 10 years. Lebanon had its last census in 1932. Almost all the countries undertook their latest censuses between 2003 and 2006. Iraq and Palestine implemented their censuses in 1997 and are expected to undertake their next round in 2007;

(b) Table 13 has been added to provide a comparison between national census population data to those estimated by the United Nations Population Division[1] in the same year. There are some differences to be noted between the actual population and the estimated figures;

(c) Population pyramids for 12 member countries are added in this issue. The country pyramids provide a comparative overview of the age distribution for women and men among the member countries. There are two distinct groups which the countries may be divided into. The first group of countries have a 'belle" shaped pyramid with a large base in some (Iraq, Jordan, Lebanon and Palestine) and a narrow top. The second group, includes the Gulf countries (Bahrain, Kuwait, Oman, Qatar, Saudi Arabia and UAE) with a skewed shape for men in the age groups 24-44. This could be attributed to the increase of working age groups of non nationals in the labor market of the Gulf countries.

---

1 Data were taken from United Nations Population Division, Department of Economic and Social Affairs (DESA), *World Population Prospects: the 2004 revision.*

يعرض القسم الأول المعنون "السكان"، بيانات عن السكان في منطقة الإسكوا ويحتوي هذا القسم على 13 جدول و12 رسم بياني عن أهرامات السكان في بلدان الأعضاء للإسكوا.

(أ) يقدم هذا العدد 12 جدول لإعطاء صورة تفصيلية حول توزيع السكان في كل من البلدان الأعضاء حسب الفئات العمرية والجنسية والجنس معتمداً على بيانات آخر تعداد أجري. باستثناء لبنان، البلد الوحيد الذي لم يُجرَ أي تعداد سكاني فيه منذ عام 1932، فإن تقريباً جميع بلدان الإسكوا تقوم بتنفيذ التعدادات السكانية كل عشر سنوات. وقد نفذت جميع الدول تعداداتها بين 2003 و 2006، ونفذت العراق وفلسطين تعدادها القائم في 1997 ومن المتوقع إجراء تعدادها القائم في 2007.

(ب) جدول 13، تمّ زيادته لعرض مقارنة بين السكان حسب آخر تعداد للبلد وحسب تقديرات شعبة السكان الأمم المتحدة[1] في نفس سنة التعداد. ويلاحظ بعض الفروقات بين بيانات التعداد والمقدّر.

(ج) وتبين الرسومات البيانية للسكان الإسكوا عشر والتي تمّ إضافتها إلى هذا العدد. مقارنة ما بين النساء والرجال حسب التوزيع العمري في بلدان الأعضاء. ويلاحظ إمكانية تقسيم البلدان إلى فريقين: تظهر أهرام بلدان الفريق الأول (مثل العراق، والأردن ولبنان وفلسطين) قاعدة عريضة ورأس ضيق. وتبين أهرام بلدان القسم الثاني والذي يمثل بلدان منطقة الخليج (البحرين والكويت وعمان وقطر والسعودية والإمارات) انحراف الهرم نحو الرجال في الفئة العمرية (44-24) ويمكن إيعاز ذلك إلى زيادة في الفئات العمرية لغير المواطنين العاملين في سوق العمل لدول الخليج.

١ استخدمت البيانات من آفاق سكان العالم (مراجعة عام 2004 الصادرة عن شعبة السكان بالأمم المتحدة، إدارة الشؤون الاقتصادية والاجتماعية في الأمم المتحدة.

جدول 1: السكان في البحرين لآخر تعداد (2001) حسب الفئات العمرية والجنسية والجنس

Table 1: Population in Bahrain, latest available census (2001) by age groups and nationality and sex

القئة العمرية	المواطنون Nationals			غير مواطنين Non-Nationals			المجموع Total		
Age group	المجموع Total	رجال Men	نساء Women	المجموع Total	رجال Men	نساء Women	المجموع Total	رجال Men	نساء Women
<1	9187	4767	4420	2224	1191	1033	11411	5958	5453
1-4	39134	19938	19196	9840	5058	4782	48974	24996	23978
5-9	50725	25666	25059	11425	5802	5623	62150	31468	30682
10-14	49160	25281	23879	9674	5033	4641	58834	30314	28520
15-19	44240	22729	21511	6755	3603	3152	50995	26332	24663
20-24	38358	19681	18677	20317	12482	7835	58675	32163	26512
25-29	30260	15303	14957	39115	27526	11589	69375	42829	26546
30-34	28577	13942	14635	43712	30823	12889	72289	44765	27524
35-39	29337	14039	15298	36078	25882	10196	65415	39921	25494
40-44	24752	11816	12936	30506	23619	6887	55258	35435	19823
45-49	18382	9489	8893	19395	15522	3873	37777	25011	12766
50-54	12041	6573	5468	9290	7521	1769	21331	14094	7237
55-59	8556	4198	4358	3700	2939	761	12256	7137	5119
60-64	7994	3822	4172	1507	1115	392	9501	4937	4564
65-69	5732	2705	3027	669	448	221	6401	3153	3248
70-74	4479	2220	2259	400	276	124	4879	2496	2383
75+	4753	2454	2299	330	186	144	5083	2640	2443
غير محدد not stated									
المجموع Total	405667	204623	201044	244937	169026	75911	650604	373649	276955

-3-

جدول 2: السكان في مصر لآخر تعداد (2006) حسب الفئات العمرية والجنسية والجنس

Table 2: Population in Egypt, latest available census (2006) by age groups, nationality and sex

الفئة العمرية	Nationals المواطنون			Non-Nationals غير مواطنين			Total المجموع		
Age group	المجموع Total	رجال Men	نساء Women	المجموع Total	رجال Men	نساء Women	المجموع Total	رجال Men	نساء Women
<1 1-4	8255404	4231397	4024007	8064	4214	3850	8263468	4235611	4027857
5-9	9181964	4744139	4437825	8439	4427	4012	9190403	4748566	4441837
10-14	9467835	4908718	4559117	8912	4574	4338	9476747	4913292	4563455
15-19	8320248	4344315	3975933	10499	5759	4740	8330747	4350074	3980673
20-24	6078656	3175297	2903359	15121	8978	6143	6093777	3184275	2909502
25-29	5249113	2517666	2731447	11854	6517	5337	5260967	2524183	2736784
30-34	4824639	2405265	2419374	11569	6218	5351	4836208	2411483	2424725
35-39	4615786	2297883	2317903	9205	5030	4175	4624991	2302913	2322078
40-44	3821425	1932096	1889329	8498	4896	3602	3829923	1936992	1892931
45-49	3215393	1675757	1539636	6522	3810	2712	3221915	1679567	1542348
50-54	2427502	1202176	1225326	5863	3567	2296	2433365	1205743	1227622
55-59	1787204	947728	839476	3817	2322	1495	1791021	950050	840971
60-64	1678025	845859	832166	3146	1814	1332	1681171	847673	833498
65-69	1120332	611359	508973						
70-74	734935	377776	357159	4185	2242	1943	2428652	1282545	1146107
75+	569200	291168	278032						
غير محدد not stated									
المجموع Total	71347661	36508599	34839062	115694	64368	51326	71463355	36572967	34890388

جدول رقم 3: السكان في العراق لآخر تعداد (1997) حسب الفئات العمرية والجنس

Table 3: Population in Iraq latest available census (1997) by age groups and sex

الفئة العمرية Age group	المجموع Total	رجال Men	نساء Women
<1	3217047	1623589	1593458
1-4	2854432	1452030	1402402
5-9	2399217	1221918	1177299
10-14	2190496	1107893	1082603
15-19	1827565	908988	918577
20-24	1595707	798681	797026
25-29	1209668	590310	619358
30-34	774636	351942	422694
35-39	800881	386930	413951
40-44	597559	283767	313792
45-49	453287	229983	223304
50-54	348567	175620	172947
55-59	241461	111716	129745
60-64	240461	109537	130924
65-69	168525	69797	98728
70-74	109019	47399	61620
75-79	73026	32687	40339
80+	67802	26713	41089
غير محدد not stated	15187	7070	8117
المجموع Total	19184543	9536570	9647973

-5-

جدول 4: السكان في الأردن لآخر تعداد (2004) حسب الفئات العمرية والجنسية والجنس

Table 4: Population in Jordan, latest available census (2004) by age groups, nationality and sex

	Total المجموع			Non-Nationals غير مواطنين			Nationals المواطنون			الفئة العمرية Age group
	المجموع Total	رجال Men	نساء Women	المجموع Total	رجال Men	نساء Women	المجموع Total	رجال Men	نساء Women	
122757	62643	60114	6965	3541	3424	115792	59102	56690	<1
527574	270573	257001	29171	14897	14274	498403	255676	242727	1-4
642871	329133	313738	31021	15833	15188	611850	313300	298550	5-9
610129	313083	297046	27767	14414	13353	582362	298669	283693	10-14
559838	287693	272145	31617	16994	14623	528221	270699	257522	15-19
540193	279600	260593	58752	31092	27660	481441	248508	232933	20-24
456261	239774	216487	59839	37311	22528	396422	202463	193959	25-29
399169	207178	191991	49409	32641	16768	349760	174537	175223	30-34
323426	167737	155689	32713	22637	10076	290713	145100	145613	35-39
241400	123945	117455	21737	15336	6401	219663	108609	111054	40-44
170456	87098	83358	13128	8935	4193	157328	78163	79165	45-49
128240	64607	63633	9518	6119	3399	118722	58488	60234	50-54
113721	55765	57956	6969	4176	2793	106752	51589	55163	55-59
98787	52084	46703	4813	2832	1981	93974	49252	44722	60-64
71823	37095	34728	2896	1598	1298	68927	35497	33430	65-69
46820	23467	23353	1799	893	906	45021	22574	22447	70-74
24268	12651	11617	885	436	449	23383	12215	11168	75-79
22060	10137	11923	753	293	460	21307	9844	11463	80+
3846	2024	1822	2521	1362	1159	1325	662	663	غير محدد not stated
5103639	2626287	2477352	392273	231340	160933	4711366	2394947	2316419	المجموع Total

-6-

Table 5: Population in Kuwait latest available census (2005) by age groups, nationality and sex

القئة العمرية / Age group	المجموع Total (Nationals) المواطنون	رجال Men	نساء Women	المجموع Total (Non-Nationals) غير مواطنين	رجال Men	نساء Women	المجموع Total	رجال Men	نساء Women
<1	117200	60353	56847	81439	42356	39083	198639	102709	95930
1-4	116589	60431	56158	70869	36575	34294	187458	97006	90452
5-9	108713	56025	52688	57480	30302	27178	166193	86327	79866
10-14	97547	49580	47967	57570	30749	26821	155117	80329	74788
15-19	79461	40151	39310	119682	73314	46368	199143	113465	85678
20-24	64284	31029	33255	214149	144236	69913	278433	175265	103168
25-29	57369	27283	30086	209913	144145	65768	267282	171428	95854
30-34	51821	24429	27392	184734	129609	55125	236555	154038	82517
35-39	44136	20795	23341	132523	93682	38841	176659	114477	62182
40-44	35407	15733	19674	92722	68682	24040	128129	84415	43714
45-49	26736	11855	14881	54828	41814	13014	81564	53669	27895
50-54	16345	5202	11143	28879	22031	6848	45224	27233	17991
55-59	14829	6876	7953	13271	9586	3685	28100	16462	11638
60-64	11293	5712	5581	6384	4257	2127	17677	9969	7708
65-69	6650	3294	3356	3065	1770	1295	9715	5064	4651
70-74	3834	2034	1800	1386	697	689	5220	2731	2489
75-79	1840	892	948	619	272	347	2459	1164	1295
80-84	1325	673	652	507	238	269	1832	911	921
85+									
غير محدد not stated	22395	8630	13765	2609	1775	834	25004	10405	14599
المجموع Total	880774	433977	446797	1332629	876090	456539	2213403	1310067	903336

جدول 6: السكان في عمان لآخر تعداد (2003) حسب الفئات العمرية والجنسية والجنس

Table 6: Population in Oman latest available census (2003) by age groups, nationality and sex

الفئة العمرية / Age group	المواطنون Nationals			غير مواطنين Non-Nationals			المجموع Total		
	المجموع Total	رجال Men	نساء Women	المجموع Total	رجال Men	نساء Women	المجموع Total	رجال Men	نساء Women
<1	43485	21884	21601	4705	2392	2313	48190	24276	23914
1-4	172044	87659	84385	22523	11437	11086	194567	99096	95471
5-9	237476	121220	116256	23446	12137	11309	260922	133357	127565
10-14	270265	137621	132644	17955	9620	8335	288220	147241	140979
15-19	255207	130466	124741	11549	6082	5467	266756	136548	130208
20-24	214260	107482	106778	38506	23493	15013	252766	130975	121791
25-29	148259	74032	74227	87222	64195	23027	235481	138227	97254
30-34	92775	47499	45276	101096	77107	23989	193871	124606	69265
35-39	73088	35741	37347	87371	68399	18972	160459	104140	56319
40-44	60976	29449	31527	71633	59122	12511	132609	88571	44038
45-49	50554	23715	26839	47149	40523	6626	97703	64238	33465
50-54	42695	20383	22312	26941	23406	3535	69636	43789	25847
55-59	31138	15935	15203	10439	8707	1732	41577	24642	16935
60-64	32048	17240	14808	4552	3485	1067	36600	20725	15875
65-69	18378	10389	7989	1691	1074	617	20069	11463	8606
70-74	16932	8959	7973	1001	588	413	17933	9547	8386
75-79	7386	3852	3534	458	238	220	7844	4090	3754
80-84	7525	3611	3914	259	141	118	7784	3752	4032
85+	6692	3191	3501	209	128	81	6901	3319	3582
غير محدد not stated	375	212	163	552	425	127	927	637	290
المجموع Total	1781558	900540	881018	559257	412699	146558	2340815	1313239	1027576

جدول 7: السكان في فلسطين لآخر تعداد (1997) حسب الفئات العمرية والجنسية والجنس

Table 7: Population in Palestine latest available census (1997) by age groups, nationality and sex

	المجموع Total			Non-Nationals غير مواطنين			المواطنون Nationals		
الفئة العمرية Age group	نساء Women	رجال Men	المجموع Total	نساء Women	رجال Men	المجموع Total	نساء Women	رجال Men	المجموع Total
<1	44944	46957	91901	9	10	19	44935	46947	91882
1-4	188653	198218	386871	47	43	90	188606	198175	386781
5-9	206252	216599	422851	45	52	97	206207	216547	422754
10-14	156278	165295	321573	56	71	127	156222	165224	321446
15-19	132604	140747	273351	232	72	304	132372	140675	273047
20-24	114339	122317	236656	525	136	661	113814	122181	235995
25-29	91941	98962	190903	485	196	681	91456	98766	190222
30-34	79168	86195	165363	328	151	479	78840	86044	164884
35-39	59345	64425	123770	233	108	341	59112	64317	123429
40-44	44284	44384	88668	238	81	319	44046	44303	88349
45-49	33471	34880	68351	164	87	251	33307	34793	68100
50-54	29907	26091	55998	107	73	180	29800	26018	55818
55-59	24386	17598	41984	72	53	125	24314	17545	41859
60-64	23117	18786	41903	64	45	109	23053	18741	41794
65-69	19694	14755	34449	42	27	69	19652	14728	34380
70-74	14007	10941	24948	36	16	52	13971	10925	24896
75-79	7813	6559	14372	22	8	30	7791	6551	14342
80-84	4444	3750	8194	13	8	21	4431	3742	8173
85-89	2013	1935	3948	18	4	22	1995	1931	3926
90-94	1382	1372	2754	2	2	4	1380	1370	2750
95+	781	773	1554	2	3	5	779	770	1549
غير محدد not stated	582	725	1307	37	30	67	545	695	1240
المجموع Total	1279405	1322264	2601669	2777	1276	4053	1276628	1320988	2597616

Data don't include that part of Jerusalem which was annexed by Israel in 1967.

البيانات لا تشمل ذلك الجزء من محافظة القدس الذي ضمته اسرائيل بعد احتلالها للضفة الغربية عام 1967.

جدول رقم 8: السكان المواطنون في قطر لآخر تعداد (2004) حسب الفئات العمرية والجنس

Table 8: National population in Qatar latest available census (2004) by age groups and sex

الفئة العمرية Age group	المواطنون Nationals		
	المجموع Total	رجال Men	نساء Women
<1	11555	5847	5708
1-4	46993	24212	22781
5-9	56234	28420	27814
10-14	52836	26687	26149
15-19	42191	22187	20004
20-24	59567	39896	19671
25-29	84053	59477	24576
30-34	94809	66976	27833
35-39	85397	61624	23773
40-44	75877	56617	19260
45-49	59119	46488	12631
50-54	37353	29738	7615
55-59	19875	15771	4104
60-64	9127	6768	2359
65-69	4309	2805	1504
70-74	2544	1619	925
75-79	1146	676	470
80+	1044	574	470
غير محدد not stated			
المجموع Total	744029	496382	247647

جدول رقم 9 : السكان في المملكة العربية السعودية، لآخر تعداد (2004) حسب الفئات العمرية والجنسية والجنس

Table 9: Population in Saudi Arabia, latest available census (2004) by age groups, nationality and sex

القئة العمرية Age group	Nationals المواطنون			Non-Nationals غير مواطنين			Total المجموع		
	المجموع Total	رجال Men	نساء Women	المجموع Total	رجال Men	نساء Women	المجموع Total	رجال Men	نساء Women
<1	417953	210963	206990	81781	41790	39991	499734	252753	246981
1-4	1702582	855047	847535	357347	181591	175756	2059929	1036638	1023291
5-9	2239835	1127253	1112582	404908	207007	197901	2644743	1334260	1310483
10-14	2237612	1081884	1155728	344227	176568	167659	2581839	1258452	1323387
15-19	1887689	948707	938982	292498	150298	142200	2180187	1099005	1081182
20-24	1546656	760146	786510	458171	298251	159920	2004827	1058397	946430
25-29	1426739	725413	701326	866862	626706	240156	2293601	1352119	941482
30-34	1144278	569152	575126	980823	709730	271093	2125101	1278882	846219
35-39	990713	492543	498170	864837	674734	190103	1855550	1167277	688273
40-44	784871	411890	372981	633890	511983	121907	1418761	923873	494888
45-49	590851	313340	277511	410923	338148	72775	1001774	651488	350286
50-54	421581	222166	199415	236649	193133	43516	658230	415299	242931
55-59	299273	146079	153194	106524	84880	21644	405797	230959	174838
60-64	260984	126594	134390	54528	39555	14973	315512	166149	149363
65-69	204458	103245	101213	24524	16678	7846	228982	119923	109059
70-74	162175	77277	84898	16218	9837	6381	178393	87114	91279
75-79	87227	49598	37629	6960	4193	2767	94187	53791	40396
80+	121863	66073	55790	9252	4788	4464	131115	70861	60254
غير محدد not stated									
المجموع Total	16527340	8287370	8239970	6150922	4269870	1881052	22678262	12557240	10121022

جدول رقم 10: السكان في سوريا لآخر تعداد (2004) حسب الفئات العمرية والجنسية والجنس

Table 10: Population in Syria latest available census (2004) by age groups, nationality and sex

القئة العمرية Age group	المواطنون Nationals		
	المجموع Total	رجال Men	نساء Women
<1	435000	227000	208000
1-4	2027000	1036000	991000
5-9	2402000	1236000	1166000
10-14	2153000	1109000	1044000
15-19	2082000	1064000	1018000
20-24	1849000	936000	913000
25-29	1431000	718000	713000
30-34	1174000	591000	583000
35-39	1013000	509000	504000
40-44	836000	427000	409000
45-49	631000	327000	304000
50-54	516000	264000	252000
55-59	365000	191000	174000
60-64	293000	146000	147000
65-69	213000	109000	104000
70-74	195000	100000	95000
75+	178000	100000	78000
غير محدد not stated			
المجموع Total	17793000	9090000	8703000

جدول رقم 11: السكان في الإمارات العربية المتحدة لآخر تعداد (2005) حسب الفئات العمرية والجنسية والجنس

Table 11: Population in United Arab Emirates, latest available census (2005) by age groups, nationality and sex

القئة العمرية / Age group	المواطنون Nationals			غير مواطنين Non-Nationals			المجموع Total		
	المجموع Total	رجال Men	نساء Women	المجموع Total	رجال Men	نساء Women	المجموع Total	رجال Men	نساء Women
<1	107430	55120	52310	174714	90497	84217	282144	145617	136527
1-4	102075	52371	49704	167321	87567	79754	269396	139938	129458
5-9	104367	53985	50382	144664	76777	67887	249031	130762	118269
10-14	108111	55575	52536	124127	65823	58304	232238	121398	110840
15-19	103437	50673	52764	330106	221350	108756	433543	272023	161520
20-24	80517	39396	41121	581248	444220	137028	661765	483616	178149
25-29	52343	25846	26497	588066	464072	123994	640409	489918	150491
30-34	41743	20189	21554	458830	366565	92265	500573	386754	113819
35-39	30999	14633	16366	310283	248093	62190	341282	262726	78556
40-44	26290	12433	13857	199501	162043	37458	225791	174476	51315
45-49	20193	10246	9947	118673	97081	21592	138866	107327	31539
50-54	14234	7893	6341	52877	43410	9467	67111	51303	15808
55-59	10725	6176	4549	16603	12632	3971	27328	18808	8520
60-64	8618	5335	3283	5841	3840	2001	14459	9175	5284
65-69	6356	3657	2699	3065	1746	1319	9421	5403	4018
70-74	2826	1621	1205	1198	576	622	4024	2197	1827
75-79	2120	1160	960	849	370	479	2969	1530	1439
80-84	1788	958	830	643	304	339	2431	1262	1169
غير محدد not stated	1323	650	673	2323	1269	1054	3646	1919	1727
المجموع Total	825495	417917	407578	3280932	2388235	892697	4106427	2806152	1300275

جدول رقم 12: السكان في اليمن لآخر تعداد (2004) حسب الفئات العمرية والجنسية والجنس

Table 12: Population in Yemen, latest available census (2004) by age groups, nationality and sex

الفئة العمرية Age group	المواطنون Nationals			غير مواطنين Non-Nationals			المجموع Total		
	المجموع Total	رجال Men	نساء Women	المجموع Total	رجال Men	نساء Women	المجموع Total	رجال Men	نساء Women
<1	518703	266634	252069	1897	917	980	520600	267551	253049
1-4	2408784	1229273	1179511	8763	4474	4289	2417547	1233747	1183800
5-9	3046792	1563176	1483616	7772	3996	3776	3054564	1567172	1487392
10-14	2861833	1509907	1351926	6930	3571	3359	2868763	1513478	1355285
15-19	2468357	1260787	1207570	7793	4126	3667	2476150	1264913	1211237
20-24	1881212	960318	920894	10449	5681	4768	1891661	965999	925662
25-29	1461724	725065	736659	9349	4571	4778	1471073	729636	741437
30-34	958992	483419	475573	7985	4078	3907	966977	487497	479480
35-39	900588	426646	473942	7193	3875	3318	907781	430521	477260
40-44	721646	351163	370483	6165	3607	2558	727811	354770	373041
45-49	580373	280817	299556	4337	2794	1543	584710	283611	301099
50-54	495541	252682	242859	3286	2055	1231	498827	254737	244090
55-59	285669	148959	136710	1797	1147	650	287466	150106	137360
60-64	323262	169675	153587	1357	731	626	324619	170406	154213
65-69	182446	96225	86221	635	335	300	183081	96560	86521
70-74	218021	113862	104159	598	279	319	218619	114141	104478
75-79	93843	50835	43008	226	105	121	94069	50940	43129
80-84	99601	51510	48091	208	74	134	99809	51584	48225
85+	78550	42151	36399	231	99	132	78781	42250	36531
غير محدد not stated	11353	6677	4676	900	657	243	12253	7334	4919
المجموع Total	19597290	9989781	9607509	87871	47172	40699	19685161	10036953	9648208

جدول رقم 13: السكان لآخر تعداد والمقدر حسب الجنس
Table 13: Population, latest available census and estimate by sex

	تاريخ التعداد Census date	سكان التعداد حسب الجنس Census Population by sex			السكان المقدرين * حسب الجنس Estimated Population* by sex		
		المجموع Total	رجال Men	نساء Women	المجموع Total	رجال Men	نساء Women
Bahrain البحرين	2001	650604	373649	276955	665000	382000	283000
Egypt مصر	2006	71463355	36572967	34890388	69939000	37136000	32803000
Iraq العراق	1997	19184543	9536570	9647973	23015000	11659000	11356000
Jordan الأردن	2004	5103639	2626287	2477352	5371000	2767000	2604000
Kuwait الكويت	2005	2213403	1310067	903336	2700000	1629000	1071000
Oman عمان	2003	2340815	1313239	1027576	2459000	1395000	1064000
Palestine فلسطين	1997(1)	2601669	1322264	1279405	2821000	1431000	1390000
Qatar قطر	2004	744029	496382	247647	764000	511000	253000
Kingdom of Saudi Arabia المملكة العربية السعودية	2004	22678262	12557240	10121022	23047000	12745000	10302000
Syrian Arab Republic الجمهورية العربية السورية	2004	17793000	9090000	8703000	18390000	9284000	9106000
United Arab Emirates الإمارات العربية المتحدة	2005	4106427	2806152	1300275	4104000	2789000	1315000
Yemen اليمن	2004	19685161	10036953	9648208	20478000	10366000	10112000

(1) Excludes uncounted population estimated according to post enumeration survey and population estimates for those parts of Jerusalem which were annexed by Israel in 1967.

* Data for the estimated population taken from World Population Prospects: 2006 Revision

(1) لا يشمل تقديرات عدد السكان الذين لم يتم عدهم على ضوء مسح ما بعد التعداد، وكذلك تقديرات عدد السكان في ذلك الجزء من محافظة القدس والذي ضمته اسرائيل بعد احتلالها للاراضي الفلسطينية عام 1967.

* يؤخذ السكان المقدرين مستمدة من افق سكان العالم: مراجعة عام 2006.

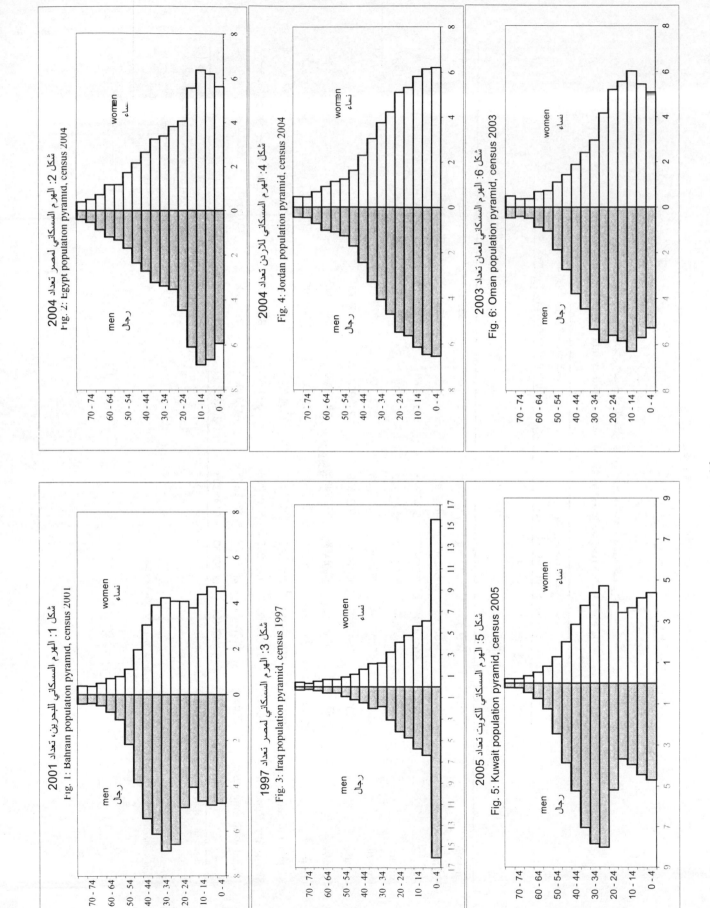

شكل 1: الهرم السكاني للبحرين تعداد 2001
Fig. 1: Bahrain population pyramid, census 2001

شكل 3: الهرم السكاني لمصر تعداد 1997
Fig. 3: Iraq population pyramid, census 1997

شكل 5: الهرم السكاني للكويت تعداد 2005
Fig. 5: Kuwait population pyramid, census 2005

شكل 2: الهرم السكاني لمصر تعداد 2004
Fig. 2: Egypt population pyramid, census 2004

شكل 4: الهرم السكاني للأردن تعداد 2004
Fig. 4: Jordan population pyramid, census 2004

شكل 6: الهرم السكاني لعمان تعداد 2003
Fig. 6: Oman population pyramid, census 2003

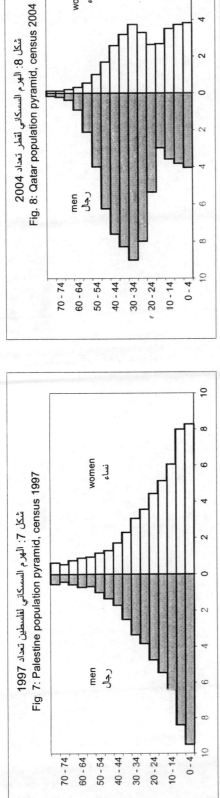

شكل الهرم السكاني لفلسطين تعداد 1997
Fig. 7: Palestine population pyramid, census 1997

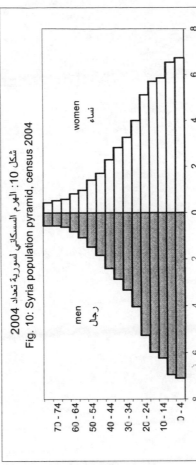

شكل 8: الهرم السكاني لقطر تعداد 2004
Fig. 8: Qatar population pyramid, census 2004

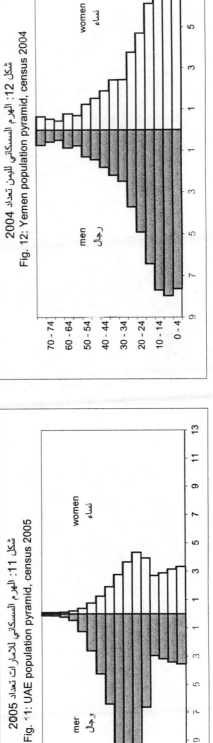

شكل 9: الهرم السكاني للسعودية تعداد 2004
Fig. 9: Saudi Arabia population pyramid, census 2004

شكل 10: الهرم السكاني لسورية تعداد 2004
Fig. 10: Syria population pyramid, census 2004

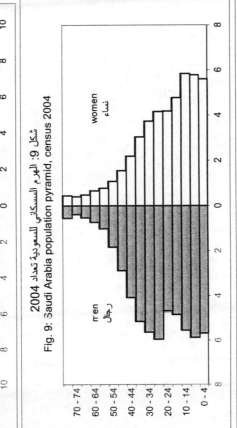

شكل 11: الهرم السكاني للإمارات تعداد 2005
Fig. 11: UAE population pyramid, census 2005

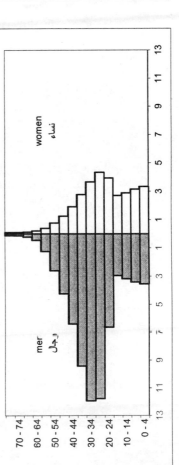

شكل 12: الهرم السكاني لليمن تعداد 2004
Fig. 12: Yemen population pyramid, census 2004

القسم الثاني
Section Two

الخصوبة والوفيات
Fertility and Mortality

Section II is on Fertility and Mortality. It presents data on births, deaths, infant deaths and causes of death in the ESCWA region from 2000 to the most recent year, for available data in each country[2]. This section contains three tables with their respective graphs.

(a) Table 14, presents the registered number of live births, total number of deaths and number of infant deaths, including the calculated crude birth rate (CBR), crude death rate (CDR), rate of natural increase (RNI) and infant mortality rate (IMR) for each member country since 2000. The Table also includes the estimated rates by the United Nations Population Division for the periods 2000-2005 and 2005-2010.

The highest CBR registered in member countries in 2005 was in Syria 36 live births per 1000 population and the lowest was in United Arab Emirates 14 live births per 1000 population. The highest CDR was recorded in Egypt at around 6 deaths per 1000 population and the lowest was in Yemen at around 1 death per 1000 population.

Four countries did not provide registered data on IMR, namely; Jordan, Lebanon, Syria and Yemen. The available data from some of the countries show a slight change in IMR during the reported period. However, major decreases in IMR were registered by Egypt and Oman (9 percentage points), followed by Palestine (5 percentage points) and Qatar (4 percentage points). The highest IMR was in Egypt at 22.6 (2004), followed by Saudi Arabia at 19 and Iraq at around 14 deaths per 1000 live births in 2005.

A bar graph in Fig. 13 presents countries' IMRs, where available, for 2000 and 2005.

(b) Table 15, presents data on registered live births, general fertility rate (GFR), total fertility rate (TFR), gross reproduction rate (GRR) and mean age of childbearing from 2000 to 2005.

TFR was reported by seven countries, namely; Bahrain, Egypt, Iraq, Kuwait, Oman, Qatar and UAE. Kuwait halved its TFR during the reported period to 2.3 births per woman. Although United Arab Emirates made some reductions in its TFR (0.9 percentage points) from 2000 to 2004 its TFR remains to be the highest among the reported countries in the region.

-20-

ويعرض الرسم البياني معدل الإجمالي للخصوبة لكل من البحرين ومصر والعراق والكويت وقطر ودولة الإمارات العربية المتحدة.

(ج) الجدول 16: يعرض بيانات عن الوفيات المسجلة حسب الجنسية والجنس، وفقاً للتصنيف الدولي للأمراض.

في عام 2005، تشير البيانات الواردة من البلدان الأعضاء إلى أن الأسباب الأكثر انتشاراً للوفاة هي أمراض الجهاز الدوري الدموي، وأمراض وحالات غير معينة و غير مشخصة في مكان آخر وكذلك إلى أمراض معدية وطفيلية معينة.

TFR for the period 1990-2005 is illustrated in six line graphs for the following countries: Bahrain, Egypt, Iraq, Kuwait, Qatar and UAE.

(c) Table 16, presents distribution of causes of death by nationality and sex classified in accordance to the International Classification of Diseases.

In 2005 the major causes of deaths in the ESCWA region are attributed to: Diseases of the circulatory system; Symptoms, signs and abnormal clinical and laboratory findings, nct elsewhere classified; and Certain infectious and parasitic diseases.

---

[2] أدرجت في الجداول فقط البلدان التي تتوافر بشأنها المعلومات، وجرى احتساب المعدلات بناء على البيانات الوطنية. للبيانات ما قبل 2000، مراجعة النشرات السابقة.

[2] Only those countries for which relevant data are available have been included in the tables, and averages have been calculated on the basis of national figures. For data before 2000, refer to the previous issues.

2000 جدول ١٤ : معدل المواليد والوفيات الخام ومعدل الزيادة الطبيعية ووفيات الرضيع المسجل والمقدر منذ عام

Table 14 : Registered and Estimated Crude Birth Rate, Crude Death Rate, Rate of Natural Increase and Infant Mortality Rate since 2000

Country / Year	Estimated Population- Medium Variant (a. b. c. d)	Registered							Estimated Rates (A,B) - Medium Variant			
		Number of Live births	Number of Deaths	Number of Infant Deaths	Crude Birth Rate (per '000)	Crude Death Rate (per '000)	Rate of Natural Increase (per '00)	Infant Mortality Rate (per '000)	Crude Birth Rate (per '000)	Crude Death Rate (per '000)	Rate of Natural Increase (per '00)	Infant Mortality Rate (per '000)
BAHRAIN [1] البحرين [1]												
2005	727000	15198	2222	134	20.9	3.1	1.8	8.8				
2005-2010 (B)	**727000**	**15198**	**2222**	**134**	**20.9**	**3.1**	**1.8**	**8.8**	**17.0**	**3.0**	**1.4**	**11.0**
2004	716000	14968	2215	141	20.9	3.1	1.8	9.4				
2003	724000	14560	2114	107	20.1	2.9	1.7	7.3				
2002	709000	13576	2035	94	19.1	2.9	1.6	6.9				
2001	652000	13468	1979	117	20.7	3.0	1.8	8.7				
2000	640000	13947	2045	117	21.8	3.2	1.9	8.4				
2000-2005 (A)	**688200**	**14104**	**2078**	**115**	**20.5**	**3.0**	**1.7**	**8.2**	**15.7**	**3.7**	**1.2**	**14.0**
EGYPT مصر												
2005	74035000	1800972	440149	...	24.3	5.9	1.8	...				
2005-2010 (B)	**74035000**	**1800972**	**440149**	**...**	**24.3**	**5.9**	**1.8**	**...**	**24.0**	**6.0**	**1.8**	**29.0**
2004	72640000	1779500	440790	40177	24.5	6.1	1.8	22.6				
2003	71931000	1777418	440149	38859	24.7	6.1	1.9	21.9				
2002	70507000	1766589	424034	37904	25.1	6.0	1.9	21.5				
2001	69080000	1741308	404531	49149	25.2	5.9	1.9	28.2				
2000	67884000	1751854	404699	55214	25.8	6.0	2.0	31.5				
2000-2005 (A)	**70408800**	**1763334**	**422841**	**44261**	**25.0**	**6.0**	**1.9**	**25.1**	**23.3**	**6.1**	**1.7**	**40.0**

[1] Include births to the nationals living abroad, and excluding late registration
[1] تشمل مواليد المواطنين المقيمين في الخارج، ولا تشمل التسجيل المتأخر.

جدول 14 (تابع) : معدل المواليد والوفيات الخام ومعدل الزيادة الطبيعية ووفيات الرضيع المسجل والمقدر منذ عام 2000

Table 14 (cont'd): Registered and Estimated Crude Birth Rate, Crude Death Rate, Rate of Natural Increase and Infant Mortality Rate since 2000

Country/ Year	Estimated Population- Medium Variant (a, b, c, d)	Registered Number of Live births	Number of Deaths	Number of Infant Deaths	Crude Birth Rate (per '000)	Crude Death Rate (per '000)	Rate of Natural Increase (per '00)	Infant Mortality Rate (per '000)	Estimated Rates (A,B) - Medium Variant: Crude Birth Rate (per '000)	Crude Death Rate (per '000)	Rate of Natural Increase (per '00)	Infant Mortality Rate (per '000)	
IRAQ العراق													
2005	28807000	896340	115775	12460	31.1	4.0	2.7	13.9					2005
2005-2010 [B]	**28807000**	**896340**	**115775**	**12460**	**31.1**	**4.0**	**2.7**	**13.9**	**32.0**	**9.0**	**2.3**	**82.0**	**[B]2010-2005**
2004	28057000	840257	101820	10972	29.9	3.6	2.6	13.1					2004
2003	25175000	691269	95935	9638	27.5	3.8	2.4	13.9					2003
2002	24510000	746771	85758	12447	30.5	3.5	2.7	16.7					2002
2001	23584000	716861	77727	…	…	…	…	…					2001
2000	22946000	471886	179928	…	20.6	7.8	1.3	…					2000
2000-2005 [A]	**24854400**	**693409**	**108234**	**11019**	**27.9**	**4.4**	**2.4**	**15.9**	**33.9**	**7.0**	**2.7**	**64.0**	**[A]2005-2000**
JORDAN الأردن [II]													**[II]**
2006	5729000	162972	20397	…	28.4	3.6	2.5	…					2006
2005	5703000	152276	17883	…	26.7	3.1	2.4	…					2005
2005-2010 [B]	**5716000**	**157624**	**19140**	…	**27.6**	**3.3**	**2.4**	…	**26.0**	**4.0**	**2.2**	**19.0**	**[B]2010-2005**
2004	5561000	150248	17011	…	27.0	3.1	2.4	…					2004
2003	5473000	148294	16937	…	27.1	3.1	2.4	…					2003
2002	5329000	146077	17220	…	27.4	3.2	2.4	…					2002
2001	5051000	142956	16164	…	28.3	3.2	2.5	…					2001
2000	4913000	126016	13339	…	25.6	2.7	2.3	…					2000
2000-2005 [A]	**5265400**	**142718**	**16134**	…	**27.1**	**3.1**	**2.4**	…	**32.8**	**4.3**	**2.9**	…	**[A]2005-2000**

[II] Excluding births to Nationals abroad.   [II] لا تشمل مواليد المواطنين المقيمين في الخارج

جدول 14 (تابع) : معدل المواليد والوفيات الخام ومعدل الزيادة الطبيعية ووفيات الرضيع المسجل والمقدر منذ عام 2000

Table 14 (cont'd): Registered and Estimated Crude Birth Rate, Crude Death Rate, Rate of Natural Increase and Infant Mortality Rate since 2000

Country/ Year	Estimated Population[1] Medium Variant (a. b. c. d)	Registered							Estimated Rates (A,B) - Medium Variant			
		Number of Live births	Number of Deaths	Number of Infant Deaths	Crude Birth Rate (per '000)	Crude Death Rate (per '000)	Rate of Natural Increase (per '00)	Infant Mortality Rate (per '000)	Crude Birth Rate (per '000)	Crude Death Rate (per '000)	Rate of Natural Increase (per '000)	Infant Mortality Rate (per '000)
KUWAIT الكويت												
2005	2687000	50941	4784	420	19.0	1.8	1.7	8.2				
2005-2010[B]	**2687000**	**50941**	**4784**	**420**	**19.0**	**1.8**	**1.7**	**8.2**	**18.0**	**2.0**	**1.6**	**8.0**
2004	2606000	47274	4793	422	18.1	1.8	1.6	8.9				
2003	2521000	43982	4424	412	17.4	1.8	1.6	9.4				
2002	2443000	43490	4342	418	17.8	1.8	1.6	9.6				
2001	1971000	41342	4364	420	21.0	2.2	1.9	10.2				
2000	1914000	41843	4227	379	21.9	2.2	2.0	9.1				
2000-2005[A]	**2291000**	**43586**	**4430**	**407**	**19.0**	**1.9**	**1.7**	**9.3**	**19.2**	**2.7**	**1.7**	**11.0**
LEBANON لبنان												
2006	4055000	82913	20544	...	20.4	5.1	1.5	...				
2005	3577000	85754	21038	...	24.0	5.9	1.8	...				
2005-2010[B]	**3816000**	**84334**	**20791**	**...**	**22.1**	**5.4**	**1.7**	**...**	**18.0**	**7.0**	**1.1**	**22.0**
2004	3540000	84622	19545	...	23.9	5.5	...	...				
2003	3653000	82215	18797	...	22.5	5.1	1.7	...				
2002	3596000	86670	18867	...	24.1	5.2	1.9	...				
2001	3556000	88027	18054	...	24.8	5.1	2.0	...				
2000	3497000	86770	18756	...	24.8	5.4	1.9	...				
2000-2005[A]	**3575500**	**85921**	**18619**	**...**	**24.0**	**5.2**	**1.9**	**...**	**19.0**	**5.4**	**1.4**	**...**

-25-

جدول 14 (تابع) : معدل المواليد والوفيات الخام ومعدل الزيادة الطبيعية ووفيات الرضيع المسجل والمقدر منذ عام 2000

Table 14 (cont'd): Registered and Estimated Crude Birth Rate, Crude Death Rate, Rate of Natural Increase and Infant Mortality Rate since 2000

Country/ Year	Estimated Population- Medium Variant [I] (a, b, c, d)	Registered							Estimated Rates (A,B) - Medium Variant			
		Number of Live births	Number of Deaths	Number of Infant Deaths	Crude Birth Rate (per '000)	Crude Death Rate (per '000)	Rate of Natural Increase (per '00)	Infant Mortality Rate (per '000)	Crude Birth Rate (per '000)	Crude Death Rate (per '000)	Rate of Natural Increase (per '00)	Infant Mortality Rate (per '000)
OMAN [IV]												
2006	1883576	45534	5187	440	24.2	2.8	2.1	9.7				
2005	1842684	45602	4995	353	24.7	2.7	2.2	7.7				
2005-2010 (B)	1863130	45568	5091	397	24.5	2.7	2.2	8.7	22.0	3.0	1.9	12.0
2004	1802931	43270	4688	358	24.0	2.6	2.1	8.3				
2003	1781558	43470	4810	448	24.4	2.7	2.2	10.3				
2002	1869580	48048	6544	778	25.7	3.5	2.2	16.2				
2001	1826124	51862	6391	840	28.4	3.5	2.5	16.2				
2000	1777685	57953	6577	968	32.6	3.7	2.9	16.7				
2000-2005 (A)	1811576	48921	5802	678	27.0	3.2	2.4	13.5	36.0	4.1	3.2	23.0
PALESTINE [V]												
2006	3889000	100853	9202	830	25.9	2.4	2.4	8.2				
2005	3702000	109439	9645	1057	29.6	2.6	2.7	9.7				
2005-2010 (B)	3795500	105146	9424	944	27.7	2.5	2.5	9.0	36.0	4.0	3.2	18.0
2004	3587000	111245	10029	1103	31.0	2.8	2.8	9.9				
2003	3557000	106356	10207	1150	29.9	2.9	2.7	10.8				
2002	3433000	106511	10162	1107	31.0	3.0	2.8	10.4				
2001	3311000	92526	9223	1343	27.9	2.8	2.5	14.5				
2000	3191000	92995	9118	1378	29.1	2.9	2.6	14.8				
2000-2005 (A)	3415800	101927	9748	1216	29.8	2.9	2.7	11.9	39.0	4.3	3.5	21.0

[IV] Population and data estimates (national sources) (for Omani only)

[V] The source for the number of deaths in this table is Ministry of Health (discrepency with the number in the table 6)

[IV] تقديرات السكان والبيانات: مصادر وطنية (للعمانيين فقط)

[V] مصدر عدد الوفيات في هذا الجدول من وزارة الصحة (وتختلف مع الرقم المذكور في الجدول 6)

جدول 14 (تابع) : معدل المواليد والوفيات الخام ومعدل الزيادة الطبيعية ووفيات الرضيع المسجل والمقدر منذ عام 2000

Table 14 (cont'd): Registered and Estimated Crude Birth Rate, Crude Death Rate, Rate of Natural Increase and Infant Mortality Rate since 2000

Country / Year	Estimated Population - Medium Variant [1] (a, b, c, d)	Registered Number of Live births	Number of Deaths	Number of Infant Deaths	Crude Birth Rate (per '000)	Crude Death Rate (per '000)	Rate of Natural Increase (per '00)	Infant Mortality Rate (per '000)	Estimated Rates [A,B] - Medium Variant Crude Birth Rate (per '000)	Crude Death Rate (per '000)	Rate of Natural Increase (per '00)	Infant Mortality Rate (per '000)
QATAR قطر												
2006	821000	14120	1750	114	17.2	2.1	1.5	8.1				
2005	813000	13401	1546	110	16.5	1.9	1.5	8.2				
2005-2010[B]	**817000**	**13761**	**1648**	**112**	**16.8**	**2.0**	**1.5**	**8.1**	**16.0**	**2.0**	**1.4**	**8.0**
2004	777000	13190	1341	113	17.0	1.7	1.5	8.6				
2003	610000	12856	1311	137	21.1	2.1	1.9	10.7				
2002	601000	12200	1220	107	20.3	2.0	1.8	8.8				
2001	575000	12118	1210	111	21.1	2.1	1.9	9.2				
2000	555000	11250	1173	141	19.9	2.1	1.8	12.5				
2000-2005[A]	**625600**	**12323**	**1251**	**122**	**19.7**	**2.0**	**1.8**	**9.9**	**17.4**	**4.1**	**1.3**	**11.0**
KINGDOM OF SAUDI ARABIA [VI] المملكة العربية السعودية												
2006	24175000	589223	93752	10954	24.4	3.9	2.0	18.6				
2005	24573000	582582	92487	11078	23.7	3.8	2.0	19.0				
2005-2010[B]	**24374000**	**585903**	**93120**	**11016**	**24.0**	**3.8**	**2.0**	**18.8**	**25.0**	**4.0**	**2.1**	**19.0**
2004	23950000	574211	91243	11164	24.0	3.8	2.0	19.4				
2003	24217000	565961	90016	11251	23.4	3.7	2.0	19.9				
2002	23520000	557828	92486	...	23.7	3.9	2.0	...				
2001	21028000	549813	91319	...	26.1	4.3	2.2	...				
2000	20346000	541913	...	...	26.6	...	...	...				
2000-2005[A]	**22611200**	**557945**	**91266**	**...**	**24.7**	**4.0**	**2.1**	**...**	**33.8**	**4.1**	**3.0**	**...**

VII Estimated vital events data — بيانات الوقعات الحيوية المقدرة VII

جدول 14 (تابع) : معدل المواليد والوفيات الخام ومعدل الزيادة الطبيعية ووفيات الرضيع المسجل والمقدر منذ عام 2000

Table 14 (cont'd): Registered and Estimated Crude Birth Rate, Crude Death Rate, Rate of Natural Increase and Infant Mortality Rate since 2000

Country/ Year	Estimated Population Medium Variant[1] (a, b, c, d)	Registered — Number of Live births	Number of Deaths	Number of Infant Deaths	Crude Birth Rate (per '000)	Crude Death Rate (per '000)	Rate of Natural Increase (per '00)	Infant Mortality Rate (per '000)	Estimated Rates (A,B) – Medium Variant — Crude Birth Rate (per '000)	Crude Death Rate (per '000)	Rate of Natural Increase (per '00)	Infant Mortality Rate (per '000)
SYRIAN ARAB REPUBLIC [VII, VIII]												
2006	...	656599	72534	...	...	...	...	...				
2005	17678479	634170	73968	...	35.9	4.2	3.2	...				
2005-2010[(B)]	**17678479**	**645385**	**73251**	...	**36.5**	**4.1**	**3.2**	...	**27.0**	**3.0**	**2.4**	**16.0**
2004	17353897	598221	68551	...	34.5	4.0	3.1	...				
2003	17119987	609774	62880	...	35.6	3.7	3.2	...				
2002	16700101	574918	62184	...	34.4	3.7	3.1	...				
2001	16336858	524212	60814	...	32.1	3.7	2.8	...				
2000	15943529	505484	57857	...	31.7	3.6	2.8	...				
2000-2005[(A)]	**16690874**	**562522**	**62457**	...	**33.7**	**3.7**	**3.0**	...	**29.6**	**4.0**	**2.6**	...
UNITED ARAB EMIRATES												
2005	4496000	64623	6361	500	14.4	1.4	1.3	7.7				
2005-2010[(B)]	**4496000**	**64623**	**6361**	**500**	**14.4**	**1.4**	**1.3**	**7.7**	**16.0**	**1.0**	**1.5**	**8.0**
2004	4284000	63113	6123	550	14.7	1.4	1.3	8.7				
2003	2995000	61185	6002	488	20.4	2.0	1.8	8.0				
2002	2937000	58070	5994	457	19.8	2.0	1.8	7.9				
2001	2654000	56136	5777	469	21.2	2.2	1.9	8.4				
2000	2606000	53686	5396	286	20.6	2.1	1.9	5.3				
2000-2005[(A)]	**3095200**	**58438**	**5858**	**450**	**18.9**	**1.9**	**1.7**	**7.7**	**15.7**	**4.0**	**1.2**	**11.0**

الجمهورية العربية السورية VIII, VII

الإمارات العربية المتحدة

جدول 14 (تابع) : معدل المواليد والوفيات الخام ومعدل الزيادة الطبيعية ووفيات الرضع المسجل والمقدر منذ عام 2000

Table 14 (cont'd): Registered and Estimated Crude Birth Rate, Crude Death Rate, Rate of Natural Increase and Infant Mortality Rate since 2000

Country/ Year	Estimated Population- Medium Variant[1] (a, b, c, d)	Registered							Estimated Rates (A,B) – Medium Variant			
		Number of Live births	Number of Deaths	Number of Infant Deaths	Crude Birth Rate (per '000)	Crude Death Rate (per '000)	Rate of Natural Increase (per '00)	Infant Mortality Rate (per '000)	Crude Birth Rate (per '000)	Crude Death Rate (per '000)	Rate of Natural Increase (per '00)	Infant Mortality Rate (per '000)
YEMEN												
2006*	21732000	275716	20607	...	12.7	0.9	1.2	...				
2005*	20975000	152792	19653	...	7.3	0.9	0.6	...				
2005-2010(B)	21353500	214254	20130	...	10.0	0.9	0.9	...	38.0	7.0	3.1	59.0
2004	20329000	153945	22235	...	7.6	1.1	0.6	...				
2003	20010000	130112	20559	...	6.5	1.0	0.5	...				
2002	19315000	189341	21162	...	9.8	1.1	0.9	...				
2001	19114000	260106	19868	...	13.6	1.0	1.3	...				
2000	18349000	252895	18441	...	13.8	1.0	1.3	...				
2000-2005(A)	19423400	197280	20453	...	10.2	1.1	0.9	...	48.8	8.3	4.1	...

1-b Data for 2000 and 2001 taken from World Population Prospects: 2000 Revision
1-c Data for 2002 and 2003 taken from World Population Prospects: 2002 Revision
1-d Data for 2004 and 2005 taken from World Population Prospects: 2004 Revision
1-d Data for 2006 taken from World Population Prospects: 2006 Revision
(A) Data for the estimated rates (2000-2005) taken from World Population Prospects: 2000 Revision
(B) Data for the estimated rates (2005-2010) taken from World Population Prospects: 2006 Revision
* The deaths data for nationals only

ب-١ بيانات بعد عام 2001 و 2000 مستندة من افاق سكان العالم : مراجعة عام 2000
ج-١ بيانات عام 2003 و 2002 مستندة من افاق سكان العالم : مراجعة عام 2002
د-١ بيانات عام 2005 و 2004 مستندة من افاق سكان العالم : مراجعة عام 2004
د-١ بيانات عام 2006 مستندة من افاق سكان العالم : مراجعة عام 2006
(A) بيانات المعدلات المقدرة (2000-2005) مستندة من افاق سكان العالم : مراجعة عام 2006
(B) بيانات المعدلات المقدرة (2005-2010) مستندة من افاق سكان العالم : مراجعة عام 2001
* بيانات الوفيات للمواطنين فقط

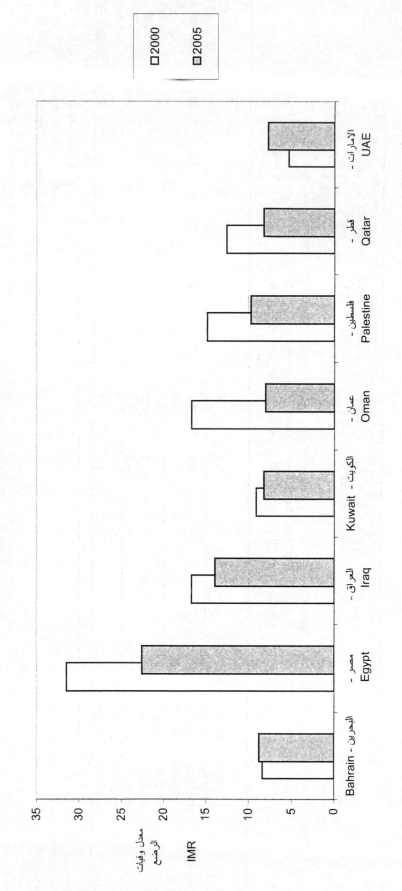

2005 و 2000 معدل وفيات الرضع في بعض بلدان الإسكوا في عام :13 شكل

Fig. 13: Infant Mortality Rate (IMR) for selected ESCWA countries in 2000 and 2005

بيانات مصر لعام 2000 و 2004
بيانات العراق لعام 2002 و 2005

Egypt data for the years 2000 and 2004
Iraq data for the years 2002 and 2005

جدول 15 : معدلات الخصوبة العام والخصوبة الكلية والإحلال الإجمالي ومتوسط عمر المرأة عند الإنجاب منذ عام 2000

Table 15[1] : General Fertility, Total Fertility and Gross Reproduction Rates, and Mean Age of Childbearing since 2000

Country/ Year	Live Births	Female Births	Mid-Year Female Population[II (a, b, c, d)]	General Fertility Rate	Total Fertility Rate (per women)	Gross Reproduction Rate (GRR) (per women)	Mean Age of Childbearing
BAHRAIN البحرين							
2005	15198	7431	173000	87.8	3.1	1.5	28.8
2004	14968	7616	178000	84.1	2.8	1.4	29.3
2003	14560	7256	174000	83.7	2.7	1.3	29.6
2002	13576	6623	171000	79.4	2.6	1.3	30.3
2001	13468	6538	180000	84.2	3.0	1.4	29.9
2000	13947	6841	156000	89.4	3.1	1.5	30.0
EGYPT مصر							
2005	1800972	981835	18699000	96.3	3.1	1.5	28.7
2004	1779500	877341	18699000	95.2	3.1	1.5	29.0
2003	1777418	877320	18583000	95.6	3.2	1.6	29.1
2002	1766589	861036	18128000	97.5	3.2	1.6	29.0
2001	1741308	846358	17711000	98.3	3.3	1.6	28.7
2000	1751854	847098	17264000	101.5	3.4	1.7	28.8
IRAQ العراق							
2000	471886	216348	5064000	93.2	3.7	1.7	30.8

-31-

جدول 15[1] (تابع): معدلات الخصوبة العام والخصوبة الكلية والاحلال الاجمالي ومتوسط عمر المرأة عند الإنجاب منذ عام 2000

Table 15[1] (cont'd): General Fertility, Total Fertility and Gross Reproduction Rates, and Mean Age of Childbearing since 2000

Country/ Year		Live Births	Female Births	Mid-Year Female Population[II (a, b, c, d)]	General Fertility Rate	Total Fertility Rate (per women)	Gross Reproduction Rate (GRR) (per women)	Mean Age of Childbearing		
KUWAIT										الكويت
	2005	50941	25019	668000	76.3	2.3	1.1	29.7	2005	
	2004	47274	23039	643000	73.5	2.2	1.1	29.6	2004	
	2003	43982	21569	604000	72.8	2.3	1.1	29.2	2003	
	2002	43490	21356	583000	74.6	2.3	1.1	29.4	2002	
	2001	41342	20316	459000	90.1	3.9	1.9	30.9	2001	
	2000	41843	20511	429000	97.5	4.3	2.1	30.8	2000	
OMAN										عمان
	2004	40529	...	472544	85.8	3.0	...	31.2	2004	
	2003	39991	...	446732	89.5	3.2	...	30.3	2003	
QATAR										قطر
	2006	14120	6924	164000	86.1	2.7	1.3	29.8	2006	
	2005	13401	6562	160000	83.8	2.8	1.3	29.8	2005	
	2004	13190	6388	154000	85.6	2.7	1.3	29.7	2004	
	2003	12856	6292	124000	103.7	4.1	2.0	29.7	2003	
	2002	12200	5939	120000	101.7	4.0	1.9	29.6	2002	
	2001	12118	5932	111000	109.2	4.3	2.1	29.7	2001	
	2000	11250	5512	108000	104.2	4.0	2.0	29.5	2000	

جدول 15¹ (تابع): معدلات الخصوبة العام والخصوبة الكلية والإجمالي الإجمالي ومتوسط عمر المرأة عند الإنجاب منذ عام 2000

Table 15¹ (cont'd): General Fertility, Total Fertility and Gross Reproduction Rates, and Mean Age of Childbearing since 2000

Country/Year	Live Births	Female Births	Mid-Year Female Population[a, b, c, d]	General Fertility Rate	Total Fertility Rate (per women)	Gross Reproduction Rate (GRR) (per women)	Mean Age of Childbearing	السنة / Year
UNITED ARAB EMIRATES								
2004	63113	30934	829000	101.9	3.5	1.7	29.7	
2003	61165	29924	600000	101.9	3.4	1.7	29.6	2003
2002	58070	28562	578000	100.5	3.4	1.7	29.6	2002
2001	56136	27518	481000	116.7	4.5	2.2	30.3	2001
2000	53686	26046	465000	115.5	4.4	2.2	30.2	2000

¹ Rates are calculated based on registered livebirths

¹-a Data for 2000 and 2001 taken from World Population Prospects: 2000 Revision

¹-b Data for 2002 and 2003 taken from World Population Prospects: 2002 Revision

¹-c Data for 2004 and 2005 taken from World Population Prospects: 2004 Revision

¹-d Data for 2006 taken from World Population Prospects: 2006 Revision

¹ احتسبت المعدلات اعتمادا على المواليد الأحياء المسجلة

¹-أ بيانات عام 2000 و 2001 مستندة من آفاق سكان العالم: مراجعة عام 2000

¹-ب بيانات عام 2002 و 2003 مستندة من آفاق سكان العالم: مراجعة عام 2002

¹-ج بيانات عام 2004 و 2005 مستندة من آفاق سكان العالم: مراجعة عام 2004

¹-د بيانات عام 2006 مستندة من آفاق سكان العالم: مراجعة عام 2006

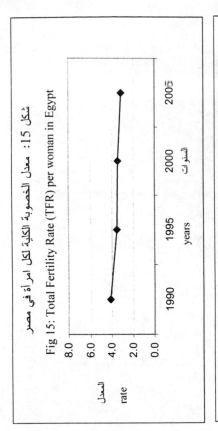

شكل 14: معدل الخصوبة الكلية لكل امرأة في البحرين

Fig 14: Total Fertility Rate (TFR) per woman in Bahrain

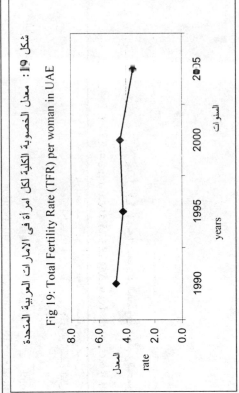

شكل 15: معدل الخصوبة الكلية لكل امرأة في مصر

Fig 15: Total Fertility Rate (TFR) per woman in Egypt

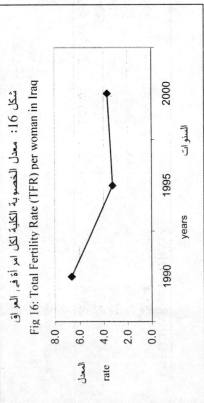
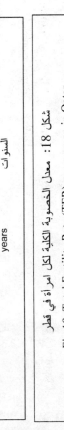

شكل 16: معدل الخصوبة الكلية لكل امرأة في العراق

Fig 16: Total Fertility Rate (TFR) per woman in Iraq

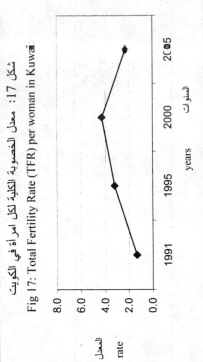

شكل 17: معدل الخصوبة الكلية لكل امرأة في الكويت

Fig 17: Total Fertility Rate (TFR) per woman in Kuwait

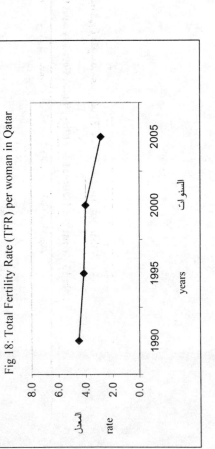

شكل 18: معدل الخصوبة الكلية لكل امرأة في قطر

Fig 18: Total Fertility Rate (TFR) per woman in Qatar

شكل 19: معدل الخصوبة الكلية لكل امرأة في الإمارات العربية المتحدة

Fig 19: Total Fertility Rate (TFR) per woman in UAE

جدول 16: أسباب الوفيات المسجلة : المعدل الخام والنسبة في المئة

Table 16: Registered Deaths by Cause: Crude Rates and Per Cent

BAHRAIN 2005 cause of death [1]	المجموع العام Grand Total			المواطنون Nationals			غير مواطنين Non-Nationals			المعدل الخام (لكل مائة ألف من السكان) Rate (per 100 thousand population)			النسبة في المئة per cent		
	مجموع Total	رجال Men	نساء Women	مجموع Total	رجال Men	نساء Women	مجموع Total	رجال Men	نساء Women	مجموع Total	رجال Men	نساء Women	مجموع Total	رجال Men	نساء Women
1	94	56	38	84	48	36	10	8	2	12.9	13.5	12.1	4.2	4.2	4.3
2	267	133	134	246	122	124	21	11	10	36.7	32.1	42.8	12.0	10.0	15.0
3	233	122	111	206	106	100	27	16	11	32.0	29.5	35.5	10.5	9.2	12.4
4	38	19	19	37	18	19	1	1	0	5.2	4.6	6.1	1.7	1.4	2.1
5	8	8	0	8	8	0	0	0	0	1.1	1.9	0.0	0.4	0.6	0.0
6	48	33	15	41	26	15	7	7	0	6.6	8.0	4.8	2.2	2.5	1.7
7	434	252	182	359	188	171	75	64	11	59.7	60.9	58.1	19.6	19.0	20.4
8	143	84	59	125	72	53	18	12	6	19.7	20.3	18.8	6.5	6.3	6.6
9	65	35	30	55	28	27	10	7	3	8.9	8.5	9.6	2.9	2.6	3.4
10	91	45	46	82	39	43	9	6	3	12.5	10.9	14.7	4.1	3.4	5.2
11	0	0	0	0	0	0	0	0	0	0.0	0.0	0.0	0.0	0.0	0.0
12	49	26	23	47	25	22	2	1	1	6.7	6.3	7.3	2.2	2.0	2.6
13	4	1	3	2	0	2	2	1	1	0.6	0.2	1.0	0.2	0.1	0.3
14	47	23	24	38	17	21	9	6	3	6.5	5.6	7.7	2.1	1.7	2.7
15	62	36	26	52	31	21	10	5	5	8.5	8.7	8.3	2.8	2.7	2.9
16	429	285	144	323	192	131	106	93	13	59.0	68.8	46.0	19.4	21.5	16.1
17	205	166	39	95	71	24	110	95	15	28.2	40.1	12.5	9.2	12.5	4.4
18	0	0	0	0	0	0	0	0	0	0.0	0.0	0.0	0.0	0.0	0.0
المجموع Total	2217	1324	893	1800	991	809	417	333	84	305.0	319.8	285.3	100.0	100.0	100.0
حجم السكان Population Size [2]	727000	414000	313000	100000			100000			100000	100000	100000			

[1] Causes of death given in annex 1 — أسباب الوفيات في الملحق رقم 1

[2] World Population Prospects - 2004 Revision. — أفاق سكان العالم – مراجعة عام 2004.

-35-

جدول 16 (تابع): المعدل الخام والنسبة في المئة : أسباب الوفيات المسجلة

Table 16 (cont'd): Registered Deaths by Cause: Crude Rates and Per Cent

BAHRAIN البحرين 2004	Grand Total المجموع العام			Nationals المواطنين			Non-Nationals غير مواطنين			Rate (per 100 thousand population) المعدل الخام (لكل مائة ألف من السكان)			per cent النسبة في المئة		
cause of death [I] سبب الوفاة	Total محموع	Men رجال	Women نساء	Total محموع	Men رجال	Women نساء	Total محموع	Men رجال	Women نساء	Total محموع	Men رجال	Women نساء	Total محموع	Men رجال	Women نساء
1	79	57	22	68	50	18	11	7	4	11.0	13.9	7.2	3.6	4.4	2.4
2	263	141	122	237	125	112	26	16	10	36.7	34.5	39.7	11.9	10.9	13.3
3	203	98	105	179	79	100	24	19	5	28.4	24.0	34.2	9.2	7.6	11.4
4	41	16	25	40	16	24	1	0	1	5.7	3.9	8.1	1.9	1.2	2.7
5	5	5	0	3	3	0	2	2	0	0.7	1.2	0.0	0.2	0.4	0.0
6	42	23	19	37	21	16	5	2	3	5.9	5.6	6.2	1.9	1.8	2.1
7	488	259	229	413	202	211	75	57	18	68.2	63.3	74.6	22.0	20.0	24.9
8	125	61	64	116	55	61	9	6	3	17.5	14.9	20.8	5.6	4.7	7.0
9	68	39	29	58	30	28	10	9	1	9.5	9.5	9.4	3.1	3.0	3.2
10	85	45	40	79	42	37	6	3	3	11.9	11.0	13.0	3.8	3.5	4.4
11	3	0	3	3	0	3	0	0	0	0.4	0.0	1.0	0.1	0.0	0.3
12	41	22	19	39	21	18	2	1	1	5.7	5.4	6.2	1.9	1.7	2.1
13	6	2	4	4	2	2	2	0	2	0.8	0.5	1.3	0.3	0.2	0.4
14	47	24	23	36	17	19	11	7	4	6.6	5.9	7.5	2.1	1.9	2.5
15	85	41	44	64	35	29	21	6	15	11.9	10.0	14.3	3.8	3.2	4.8
16	435	296	139	339	218	121	96	78	18	60.8	72.4	45.3	19.6	22.8	15.1
17	199	167	32	87	68	19	112	99	13	27.8	40.8	10.4	9.0	12.9	3.5
18	0	0	0	0	0	0	0	0	0	0.0	0.0	0.0	0.0	0.0	0.0
المجموع Total	2215	1296	919	1802	984	818	413	312	101	309.4	316.9	299.3	100.0	100.0	100.0
حجم السكان Population Size [II]	716000	409000	307000							100000	100000	100000			

[I] Causes of death given in annex I — أسباب الوفيات في الملحق رقم 1

[II] "World Population Prospects - 2004 Revision." — "آفاق سكان العالم - مراجعة عام 2004."

جدول 16 (تابع) : أسباب الوفيات المسجلة : المعدل الخام والنسبة في المئة

Table 16 (cont'd): Registered Deaths by Cause: Crude Rates and Per Cent

البحرين BAHRAIN — 2003

سبب الوفاة cause of death	المجموع العام Grand Total محموع Total	رجال Men	نساء Women	المواطنون Nationals محموع Total	رجال Men	نساء Women	غير المواطنين Non-Nationals محموع Total	رجال Men	نساء Women	المعدل الخام Rate (per 100 thousand population) محموع Total	رجال Men	نساء Women	النسبة في المئة percent محموع Total	رجال Men	نساء Women
1	82	54	28	72	48	24	10	6	4	11.3	13.0	9.1	3.9	4.3	3.2
2	271	150	121	243	134	109	28	16	12	37.4	36.1	39.3	12.8	12.1	13.9
3	168	85	83	146	69	77	22	16	6	23.2	20.4	26.9	7.9	6.8	9.5
4	39	22	17	38	22	16	1	0	1	5.4	5.3	5.5	1.8	1.8	1.9
5	1	1	0	0	0	0	1	1	0	0.1	0.2	0.0	0.0	0.1	0.0
6	36	19	17	30	15	15	6	4	2	5.0	4.6	5.5	1.7	1.5	1.9
7	597	328	269	484	239	245	113	89	24	82.5	78.8	87.3	28.2	26.4	30.8
8	143	93	50	128	79	49	15	14	1	19.8	22.4	16.2	6.8	7.5	5.7
9	95	53	42	83	44	39	12	9	3	13.1	12.7	13.6	4.5	4.3	4.8
10	76	38	38	68	31	37	8	7	1	10.5	9.1	12.3	3.6	3.1	4.4
11	3	0	3	3	0	3	0	0	0	0.4	0.0	1.0	0.1	0.0	0.3
12	45	19	26	44	19	25	1	0	1	6.2	4.6	8.4	2.1	1.5	3.0
13	0	0	0	0	0	0	0	0	0	0.0	0.0	0.0	0.0	0.0	0.0
14	52	31	21	45	26	19	7	5	2	7.2	7.5	6.8	2.5	2.5	2.4
15	43	19	24	43	19	24	0	0	0	5.9	4.6	7.8	2.0	1.5	2.8
16	236	140	96	227	136	91	9	4	5	32.6	33.7	31.2	11.2	11.3	11.0
17	44	35	9	0	0	0	44	35	9	6.1	8.4	2.9	2.1	2.8	1.0
18	183	155	28	84	73	11	99	82	17	25.3	37.3	9.1	8.7	12.5	3.2
المجموع Total	2114	1242	872	1738	954	784	376	288	88	292.0	298.6	283.1	100.0	100.0	100.0
حجم السكان Population Size [II]	724000	416000	308000							100000	100000	100000			

[I] Causes of death given in annex 1
[II] World Population Prospects - 2002 Revision.

[1] أسباب الوفيات في الملحق رقم 1
آفاق سكان العالم – مراجعة عام 2002.

جدول 16 (تابع): أسباب الوفيات المسجلة : المعدل الخام والنسبة في المئة

Table 16 (cont'd): Registered Deaths by Cause: Crude Rates and Per Cent

BAHRAIN 2002

سبب الوفاة [I] cause of death [I]	المجموع العام Grand Total			المواطنون Nationals			غير مواطنين Non-Nationals			المعدل الخام (لكل مائة ألف من السكان) Rate (per 100 thousand population)			النسبة في المئة Percent		
	مجموع Total	رجال Men	نساء Women	مجموع Total	رجال Men	نساء Women	مجموع Total	رجال Men	نساء Women	مجموع Total	رجال Men	نساء Women	مجموع Total	رجال Men	نساء Women
1	68	45	23	55	35	20	13	10	3	9.6	11.0	7.6	3.3	3.6	2.9
2	278	172	106	260	160	100	18	12	6	39.2	42.2	35.2	13.7	13.9	13.3
3	189	114	75	162	93	69	27	21	6	26.7	27.9	24.9	9.3	9.2	9.4
4	35	20	15	33	19	14	2	1	1	4.9	4.9	5.0	1.7	1.6	1.9
5	2	1	1	2	1	1	0	0	0	0.3	0.2	0.3	0.1	0.1	0.1
6	37	24	13	33	23	10	4	1	3	5.2	5.9	4.3	1.8	1.9	1.6
7	581	358	223	460	252	208	121	106	15	81.9	87.7	74.1	28.6	28.9	28.0
8	121	70	51	103	58	45	18	12	6	17.1	17.2	16.9	5.9	5.6	6.4
9	70	48	22	59	41	18	11	7	4	9.9	11.8	7.3	3.4	3.9	2.8
10	51	26	25	43	19	24	8	7	1	7.2	6.4	8.3	2.5	2.1	3.1
11	3	0	3	2	0	2	1	0	1	0.4	0.0	1.0	0.1	0.0	0.4
12	30	11	19	30	11	19	0	0	0	4.2	2.7	6.3	1.5	0.9	2.4
13	1	1	0	1	1	0	0	0	0	0.1	0.2	0.0	0.0	0.1	0.0
14	45	20	25	33	15	18	12	5	7	6.3	4.9	8.3	2.2	1.6	3.1
15	42	22	20	35	18	17	7	4	3	5.9	5.4	6.6	2.1	1.8	2.5
16	304	169	135	272	144	128	32	25	7	42.9	41.4	44.9	14.9	13.6	17.0
17	0	0	0	0	0	0	0	0	0	0.0	0.0	0.0	0.0	0.0	0.0
18	178	138	40	89	61	28	89	77	12	25.1	33.8	13.3	8.7	11.1	5.0
المجموع Total	2035	1239	796	1672	951	721	363	288	75	287.0	303.7	264.5	100.0	100.0	100.0
حجم السكان [II] Population Size [II]	709000	408000	301000							100000	100000	100000			

[I] أسباب الوفيات في الملحق رقم 1
[I] Causes of death given in annex 1

[II] آفاق سكان العالم – مراجعة عام 2005.
[II] World Population Prospects - 2002 Revision.

جدول 16 (تابع) : أسباب الوفيات المسجلة : المعدل الخام والنسبة في المئة

Table 16 (cont'd): Registered Deaths by Cause: Crude Rates and Per Cent

cause of death [1]	Grand Total — Total	Men	Women	Nationals — Total	Men	Women	Non-Nationals — Total	Men	Women	Rate (per 100 thousand population) — Total	Men	Women	percent — Total	Men	Women
1	49	31	18	41	25	16	8	6	2	7.5	8.3	6.5	2.5	2.6	2.3
2	242	146	96	211	128	83	31	18	13	37.2	39.0	34.7	12.2	12.1	12.5
3	163	96	67	154	88	66	9	8	1	25.0	25.7	24.2	8.2	7.9	8.7
4	25	12	13	23	11	12	2	1	1	3.8	3.2	4.7	1.3	1.0	1.7
5	5	5	0	4	4	0	1	1	0	0.8	1.3	0.0	0.3	0.4	0.0
6	36	17	19	29	13	16	7	4	3	5.5	4.5	6.9	1.8	1.4	2.5
7	565	359	206	412	234	178	153	125	28	86.8	96.0	74.4	28.5	29.7	26.7
8	106	62	44	98	55	43	8	7	1	16.3	16.6	15.9	5.4	5.1	5.7
9	63	36	27	55	32	23	8	4	4	9.7	9.6	9.7	3.2	3.0	3.5
10	54	28	26	46	24	22	8	4	4	8.3	7.5	9.4	2.7	2.3	3.4
11	3	0	3	2	0	2	1	0	1	0.5	0.0	1.1	0.2	0.0	0.4
12	42	17	25	38	16	22	4	1	3	6.5	4.5	9.0	2.1	1.4	3.2
13	0	0	0	0	0	0	0	0	0	0.0	0.0	0.0	0.0	0.0	0.0
14	66	38	28	49	27	22	17	11	6	10.1	10.2	10.1	3.3	3.1	3.6
15	51	31	20	39	24	15	12	7	5	7.8	8.3	7.2	2.6	2.6	2.6
16	325	175	150	298	158	140	27	17	10	49.9	46.8	54.2	16.4	14.5	19.5
17	0	0	0	0	0	0	0	0	0	0.0	0.0	0.0	0.0	0.0	0.0
18	184	155	29	95	77	18	89	78	11	28.3	41.4	10.5	9.3	12.8	3.8
Total	1979	1208	771	1594	916	678	385	292	93	304.0	323.0	278.3	100.0	100.0	100.0
Population Size [II]	651000	374000	277000							100000	100000	100000			

[1] Causes of death given in annex 1 / أسباب الوفيات في الملحق رقم 1

[II] World Population Prospects - 2000 Revision. / آفاق سكان العالم - مراجعة عام 2000.

جدول 16 (تابع) : أسباب الوفيات المسجلة : المعدل الخام والنسبة في المئة

Table 16 (cont'd): Registered Deaths by Cause: Crude Rates and Per Cent

BAHRAIN 2000 cause of death [1]	المجموع العام Grand Total			المواطنين Nationals			غير مواطنين Non-Nationals			المعدل الخام (لكل مائة ألف من السكان) Rate (per 100 thousand population)			النسبة في المئة percent		
	مجموع Total	رجال Men	نساء Women	مجموع Total	رجال Men	نساء Women	مجموع Total	رجال Men	نساء Women	مجموع Total	رجال Men	نساء Women	مجموع Total	رجال Men	نساء Women
1	85	54	31	71	43	28	14	11	3	13.3	14.7	11.4	4.2	4.4	3.7
2	247	128	119	216	111	105	31	17	14	38.6	34.8	43.8	12.1	10.5	14.4
3	140	79	61	119	64	55	21	15	6	21.9	21.5	22.4	6.8	6.5	7.4
4	19	9	10	17	8	9	2	1	1	3.0	2.4	3.7	0.9	0.7	1.2
5	6	5	1	4	3	1	2	2	0	0.9	1.4	0.4	0.3	0.4	0.1
6	28	17	11	20	11	9	8	6	2	4.4	4.6	4.0	1.4	1.4	1.3
7	536	321	215	420	223	197	116	98	18	83.8	87.2	79.0	26.2	26.4	25.9
8	84	48	36	72	42	30	12	6	6	13.1	13.0	13.2	4.1	3.9	4.3
9	73	37	36	65	30	35	8	7	1	11.4	10.1	13.2	3.6	3.0	4.3
10	54	24	30	52	22	30	2	2	0	8.4	6.5	11.0	2.6	2.0	3.6
11	2	0	2	1	0	1	1	0	1	0.3	0.0	0.7	0.1	0.0	0.2
12	39	21	18	4	2	2	35	19	16	6.1	5.7	6.6	1.9	1.7	2.2
13	3	1	2	2	0	2	1	1	0	0.5	0.3	0.7	0.1	0.1	0.2
14	50	28	22	43	24	19	7	4	3	7.8	7.6	8.1	2.4	2.3	2.7
15	58	35	23	41	25	16	17	10	7	9.1	9.5	8.5	2.8	2.9	2.8
16	261	196	65	90	70	20	171	126	45	40.8	53.3	23.9	12.8	16.1	7.8
17	49	41	8	26	21	5	23	20	3	7.7	11.1	2.9	2.4	3.4	1.0
18	311	172	139	278	149	129	33	23	10	48.6	46.7	51.1	15.2	14.1	16.8
المجموع Total	2045	1216	829	1541	848	693	504	368	136	319.5	330.4	304.8	100.0	100.0	100.0
حجم السكان Population Size [II]	640000	368000	272000							100000	100000	100000			

[1] Causes of death given in annex I
[II] "World Population Prospects - The 2000 Revision.

[1] أسباب الوفيات في الملحق رقم 1
[II] "آفاق سكان العالم - مراجعة عام 2000.

جدول 16 (تابع) : المعدل الخام والنسبة في المئة : أسباب الوفيات المسجلة

Table 16 (cont'd): Registered Deaths by Cause: Crude Rates and Per Cent

مصر EGYPT — **2005**

سبب الوفاة cause of death	المجموع العام Grand Total مجموع Total	رجال Men	نساء Women	المواطنون Nationals مجموع Total	رجال Men	نساء Women	غير مواطنين Non-Nationals مجموع Total	رجال Men	نساء Women	المعدل الخام (لكل مائة ألف من السكان) Rate (per 100 thousand population) مجموع Total	رجال Men	نساء Women	النسبة في المئة percent مجموع Total	رجال Men	نساء Women
1	14379	7897	6982	...	...	...	...	...	...	20.1	21.3	18.9	3.4	3.3	3.5
2	24168	13757	10411	...	...	...	...	...	...	32.6	37.1	28.2	5.5	5.8	5.1
3	15977	7369	8608	...	...	...	...	...	...	21.6	19.9	23.3	3.6	3.1	4.3
4	1180	569	611	...	...	...	...	...	...	1.6	1.5	1.7	0.3	0.2	0.3
5	1037	569	468	...	...	...	...	...	...	1.4	1.5	1.3	0.2	0.2	0.2
6	7210	3840	3370	...	...	...	...	...	...	9.7	10.3	9.1	1.6	1.6	1.7
7	184007	94954	89053	...	...	...	...	...	...	248.5	255.8	241.3	41.8	39.9	44.0
8	33053	17311	15742	...	...	...	...	...	...	44.6	46.6	42.6	7.5	7.3	7.8
9	38314	24325	13989	...	...	...	...	...	...	51.8	65.5	37.9	8.7	10.2	6.9
10	15971	9206	6765	...	...	...	...	...	...	21.6	24.8	18.3	3.6	3.9	3.3
11	1108	0	1108	...	...	...	...	...	...	1.5	0.0	3.0	0.3	0.0	0.5
12	159	69	90	...	...	...	...	...	...	0.2	0.2	0.2	0.0	0.0	0.0
13	2219	971	1248	...	...	...	...	...	...	3.0	2.6	3.4	0.5	0.4	0.6
14	6354	3291	3063	...	...	...	...	...	...	8.6	8.9	8.3	1.4	1.4	1.5
15	9831	5607	4224	...	...	...	...	...	...	13.3	15.1	11.4	2.2	2.4	2.1
16	66782	35247	31535	...	...	...	...	...	...	90.2	95.0	85.4	15.2	14.8	15.6
17	7503	5773	1730	...	...	...	...	...	...	10.1	15.6	4.7	1.7	2.4	0.9
18	10397	7112	3285	...	...	...	...	...	...	14.0	19.2	8.9	2.4	3.0	1.6
19	0	0	0	...	...	...	...	...	...	0.0	0.0	0.0	0.0	0.0	0.0
20	0	0	0	...	...	...	...	...	...	0.0	0.0	0.0	0.0	0.0	0.0
المجموع Total	440149	237867	202282	...	...	...	...	...	...	594.5	640.8	548.0	100.0	100.0	100.0
حجم السكان Population Size	74033000	37120000	36913000							100000.0	100000.0	100000.0			

¹ أسباب الوفاة في الملحق رقم 1 — Causes of death given in annex 1
ⁱⁱ World Population Prospects - 2004 Revision — آفاق سكان العالم – مراجعة عام 2004.

-41-

جدول 16 (تابع): أسباب الوفيات المسجلة : المعدل الخام والنسبة في المئة

Table 16 (cont'd): Registered Deaths by Cause: Crude Rates and Per Cent

سبب الوفاة cause of death [1]	المجموع العام Grand Total			المواطنون Nationals			غير مواطنين Non-Nationals			المعدل الخام (لكل مائة ألف من السكان) Rate (per 100 thousand population)			النسبة في المئة Percent		
	مجموع Total	رجال Men	نساء Women	مجموع Total	رجال Men	نساء Women	مجموع Total	رجال Men	نساء Women	مجموع Total	رجال Men	نساء Women	مجموع Total	رجال Men	نساء Women
1	15006	8125	6881	...	...	...	...	...	...	20.7	22.3	19.0	3.4	3.4	3.5
2	26608	15455	11153	...	...	...	...	...	...	36.6	42.4	30.8	6.0	6.4	5.6
3	18832	9110	9722	...	...	...	...	...	...	25.9	25.0	26.9	4.3	3.8	4.9
4	857	410	447	...	...	...	...	...	...	1.2	1.1	1.2	0.2	0.2	0.2
5	695	333	362	...	...	...	...	...	...	1.0	0.9	1.0	0.2	0.1	0.2
6	7778	4027	3751	...	...	...	...	...	...	10.7	11.1	10.4	1.8	1.7	1.9
7	185321	97079	88242	...	...	...	...	...	...	255.1	266.4	243.7	42.0	40.1	44.4
8	32497	16934	15563	...	...	...	...	...	...	44.7	46.5	43.0	7.4	7.0	7.8
9	42490	27046	15444	...	...	...	...	...	...	58.5	74.2	42.7	9.6	11.2	7.8
10	17096	10201	6895	...	...	...	...	...	...	23.5	28.0	19.0	3.9	4.2	3.5
11	379	0	379	...	...	...	...	...	...	0.5	0.0	1.0	0.1	0.0	0.2
12	206	84	122	...	...	...	...	...	...	0.3	0.2	0.3	0.0	0.0	0.1
13	4776	2287	2489	...	...	...	...	...	...	6.6	6.3	6.9	1.1	0.9	1.3
14	6332	3385	2947	...	...	...	...	...	...	8.7	9.3	8.1	1.4	1.4	1.5
15	8454	4825	3629	...	...	...	...	...	...	11.6	13.2	10.0	1.9	2.0	1.8
16	51914	26903	25011	...	...	...	...	...	...	71.5	73.8	69.1	11.8	11.1	12.6
17	7003	5512	1491	...	...	...	...	...	...	9.6	15.1	4.1	1.6	2.3	0.7
18	14546	10265	4281	...	...	...	...	...	...	20.0	28.2	11.8	3.3	4.2	2.2
المجموع Total	440790	241981	198809	...	...	...	...	...	...	606.8	664.1	549.1	100.0	100.0	100.0
حجم السكان Population Size [II]	72643000	36437000	36206000							100000	100000	100000	100000	100000	100000

[1] Causes of death given in annex I
[II] "World Population Prospects - 2004 Revision.

أسباب الوفيات في الملحق [1]
آفاق سكان العالم – مراجعة عام 2004.

-42-

Table 16 (cont'd): Registered Deaths by Cause: Crude Rates and Per Cent

cause of death [I] سبب الوفاة	Grand Total المجموع العام			Nationals المواطنون			Non-Nationals غير مواطنين			Rate (per 100 thousand population) المعدل الخام (لكل مائة ألف من السكان)			percent النسبة في المئة		
	Total مجموع	Men رجال	Women نساء	Total مجموع	Men رجال	Women نساء	Total مجموع	Men رجال	Women نساء	Total مجموع	Men رجال	Women نساء	Total مجموع	Men رجال	Women نساء
1	14879	7897	6982	...	...	...	...	...	...	20.7	22.0	19.4	3.4	3.3	3.5
2	24168	13757	10411	...	...	...	...	...	...	33.6	38.3	28.9	5.5	5.8	5.1
3	1180	569	611	...	...	...	...	...	...	22.2	20.5	23.9	0.3	0.2	0.3
4	15977	7369	8608	...	...	...	...	...	...	1.6	1.6	1.7	3.6	3.1	4.3
5	1037	569	468	...	...	...	...	...	...	1.4	1.6	1.3	0.2	0.2	0.2
6	7210	3840	3370	...	...	...	...	...	...	10.0	10.7	9.4	1.6	1.6	1.7
7	61	37	24	...	...	...	...	...	...	0.1	0.1	0.1	0.0	0.0	0.0
8	78	48	30	...	...	...	...	...	...	0.1	0.1	0.1	0.0	0.0	0.0
9	184007	94954	89053	...	...	...	...	...	...	255.8	264.5	247.1	41.8	39.9	44.0
10	33053	17311	15742	...	...	...	...	...	...	46.0	48.2	43.7	7.5	7.3	7.8
11	38314	24325	13989	...	...	...	...	...	...	53.3	67.8	38.8	8.7	10.2	6.9
12	159	69	90	...	...	...	...	...	...	0.2	0.2	0.2	0.0	0.0	0.0
13	2219	971	1248	...	...	...	...	...	...	3.1	2.7	3.5	0.5	0.4	0.6
14	15971	9206	6765	...	...	...	...	...	...	22.2	25.6	18.8	3.6	3.9	3.3
15	1108	0	1108	...	...	...	...	...	...	1.5	0.0	3.1	0.3	0.0	0.5
16	9831	5607	4224	...	...	...	...	...	...	13.7	15.6	11.7	2.2	2.4	2.1
17	6354	3291	3063	...	...	...	...	...	...	8.8	9.2	8.5	1.4	1.4	1.5
18	66643	35162	31481	...	...	...	...	...	...	92.6	97.9	87.4	15.1	14.8	15.6
19	0	0	0	...	...	...	...	...	...	0.0	0.0	0.0	0.0	0.0	0.0
20	17900	12885	5015	...	...	...	...	...	...	24.9	35.9	13.9	0.0	0.0	0.0
Total المجموع	440169	237867	202282	...	...	...	...	...	...	611.9	662.6	561.4	100.0	100.0	100.0
Population Size [II] حجم السكان	71931000	35899000	36032000							100000	100000	100000			

EGYPT مصر — **2003**

[I] Causes of death given in annex 1 — أسباب الوفيات في الملحق رقم 1

[II] World Population Prospects - 2002 Revision. — آفاق سكان العالم - مراجعة عام 2002.

جدول 16 (تابع) : أسباب الوفيات المسجلة : المعدل الخام والنسبة في المئة

Table 16 (cont'd): Registered Deaths by Cause: Crude Rates and Per Cent

مصر EGYPT 2002 سبب الوفاة cause of death [1]	المجموع العام Grand Total			المواطنون Nationals			غير المواطنين Non-Nationals			المعدل الخام (لكل مائة ألف من السكان) Rate (per 100 thousand population)			النسبة في المئة percent		
	محموع Total	رجال Men	نساء Women	محموع Total	رجال Men	نساء Women	محموع Total	رجال Men	نساء Women	محموع Total	رجال Men	نساء Women	محموع Total	رجال Men	نساء Women
1	14747	7697	7050	...	...	...	...	...	...	20.9	21.9	20.0	3.5	3.4	3.6
2	21212	12040	9172	...	...	...	...	...	...	30.1	34.2	26.0	5.0	5.3	4.7
3	13470	6037	7433	...	...	...	...	...	...	19.1	17.2	21.0	3.2	2.7	3.8
4	1677	933	744	...	...	...	...	...	...	2.4	2.7	2.1	0.4	0.4	0.4
5	897	488	409	...	...	...	...	...	...	1.3	1.4	1.2	0.2	0.2	0.2
6	5490	2948	2542	...	...	...	...	...	...	7.8	8.4	7.2	1.3	1.3	1.3
7	179200	92218	86982	...	...	...	...	...	...	254.2	262.1	246.3	42.3	40.7	44.1
8	30077	15797	14280	...	...	...	...	...	...	42.7	44.9	40.4	7.1	7.0	7.2
9	33877	20928	12949	...	...	...	...	...	...	48.0	59.5	36.7	8.0	9.2	6.6
10	15622	8914	6708	...	...	...	...	...	...	22.2	25.3	19.0	3.7	3.9	3.4
11	781	0	781	...	...	...	...	...	...	1.1	0.0	2.2	0.2	0.0	0.4
12	158	82	76	...	...	...	...	...	...	0.2	0.2	0.2	0.0	0.0	0.0
13	313	128	185	...	...	...	...	...	...	0.4	0.4	0.5	0.1	0.1	0.1
14	5966	3145	2821	...	...	...	...	...	...	8.5	8.9	8.0	1.4	1.4	1.4
15	14265	7619	6646	...	...	...	...	...	...	20.2	21.7	18.8	3.4	3.4	3.4
16	66918	34547	32371	...	...	...	...	...	...	94.9	98.2	91.7	15.8	15.2	16.4
17	7380	5757	1623	...	...	...	...	...	...	10.5	16.4	4.6	1.7	2.5	0.8
18	11984	7532	4452	...	...	...	...	...	...	17.0	21.4	12.6	2.8	3.3	2.3
المجموع Total	424034	226810	197224	...	...	...	...	...	...	601.4	644.6	558.4	100.0	100.0	100.0
حجم السكان Population Size [2]	70507000	35188000	35319000							100000	100000	100000			

[1] Causes of death given in annex 1 — أسباب الوفيات في الملحق _ قم 1

[2] World Population Prospects - 2002 Revision. — أفق سكان العالم - مراجعة عام 2002.

جدول 16 (تابع) : أسباب الوفيات المسجلة : المعدل الخام والنسبة في المئة
Table 16 (cont'd): Registered Deaths by Cause: Crude Rates and Per Cent

EGYPT / 2001

سبب الوفاة [1] cause of death	المجموع العام Grand Total			المواطنون Nationals			غير مواطنين Non-Nationals			المعدل الخام (لكل مائة ألف من السكان) Rate (per 100 thousand population)			النسبة في المئة percent		
	مجموع Total	رجال Men	نساء Women	مجموع Total	رجال Men	نساء Women	مجموع Total	رجال Men	نساء Women	مجموع Total	رجال Men	نساء Women	مجموع Total	رجال Men	نساء Women
1	13592	7602	5990	...	...	...	...	...	...	19.7	21.7	17.6	3.4	3.4	3.3
2	19635	11389	8246	...	...	...	...	...	...	28.4	32.6	24.2	4.9	5.1	4.5
3	11915	5546	6369	...	...	...	...	...	...	17.2	15.9	18.7	2.9	2.5	3.5
4	2225	1315	910	...	...	...	...	...	...	3.2	3.8	2.7	0.6	0.6	0.5
5	1669	948	721	...	...	...	...	...	...	2.4	2.7	2.1	0.4	0.4	0.4
6	5805	3309	2496	...	...	...	...	...	...	8.4	9.5	7.3	1.4	1.5	1.4
7	174434	92363	82071	...	...	...	...	...	...	252.5	264.2	240.6	43.1	41.4	45.2
8	31186	16654	14532	...	...	...	...	...	...	45.1	47.6	42.6	7.7	7.5	8.0
9	30909	19891	11018	...	...	...	...	...	...	44.7	56.9	32.3	7.6	8.9	6.1
10	14023	8328	5695	...	...	...	...	...	...	20.3	23.8	16.7	3.5	3.7	3.1
11	1200	0	1200	...	...	...	...	...	...	1.7	0.0	3.5	0.3	0.0	0.7
12	375	261	114	...	...	...	...	...	...	0.5	0.7	0.3	0.1	0.1	0.1
13	327	165	162	...	...	...	...	...	...	0.5	0.5	0.5	0.1	0.1	0.1
14	6266	3327	2939	...	...	...	...	...	...	9.1	9.5	8.6	1.5	1.5	1.6
15	13039	7243	5796	...	...	...	...	...	...	18.9	20.7	17.0	3.2	3.2	3.2
16	57670	30434	27236	...	...	...	...	...	...	83.5	87.0	79.8	14.3	13.7	15.0
17	8065	5552	2513	...	...	...	...	...	...	11.7	15.9	7.4	2.0	2.5	1.4
18	12196	8604	3592	...	...	...	...	...	...	17.7	24.6	10.5	3.0	3.9	2.0
المجموع Total	404531	222931	181600	...	...	...	...	...	...	585.6	637.6	532.3	100.0	100.0	100.0
حجم السكان [II] Population Size	69080000	34965000	34115000	100000	100000	100000									

[1] أسباب الوفيات في الملحق رقم 1
[1] Causes of death given in annex 1

[II] أسباب الوفيات في العالم – مراجعة عام 2000.
[II] "World Population Prospects - 2000 Revision."

جدول 16 (تابع) : أسباب الوفيات المسجلة : المعدل الخام والنسبة في المئة

Table 16 (cont'd): Registered Deaths by Cause: Crude Rates and Per Cent

مصر EGYPT 2000

سبب الوفاة cause of death [1]	المجموع العام Grand Total			المواطنون Nationals			غير مواطنين Non-Nationals			المعدل الخام (لكل مائة ألف من السكان) Rate (per 100 thousand population)			النسبة في المئة percent		
	مجموع Total	رجال Men	نساء Women	مجموع Total	رجال Men	نساء Women	مجموع Total	رجال Men	نساء Women	مجموع Total	رجال Men	نساء Women	مجموع Total	رجال Men	نساء Women
1	20652	11207	9445	...	...	...	...	...	...	30.4	32.6	28.2	5.1	5.1	5.2
2	20496	11930	8566	...	...	...	...	...	...	30.2	34.7	25.6	5.1	5.4	4.7
3	11215	5030	6185	...	...	...	...	...	...	16.5	14.6	18.5	2.8	2.3	3.4
4	1093	591	502	...	...	...	...	...	...	1.6	1.7	1.5	0.3	0.3	0.3
5	479	231	248	...	...	...	...	...	...	0.7	0.7	0.7	0.1	0.1	0.1
6	5086	2786	2300	...	...	...	...	...	...	7.5	8.1	6.9	1.3	1.3	1.3
7	174511	91826	82685	...	...	...	...	...	...	257.1	267.2	246.7	43.1	41.5	45.1
8	37498	19739	17759	...	...	...	...	...	...	55.2	57.4	53.0	9.3	8.9	9.7
9	29568	18815	10753	...	...	...	...	...	...	43.6	54.8	32.1	7.3	8.5	5.9
10	13522	8015	5507	...	...	...	...	...	...	19.9	23.3	16.4	3.3	3.6	3.0
11	532	0	532	...	...	...	...	...	...	0.8	0.0	1.6	0.1	0.0	0.3
12	99	58	41	...	...	...	...	...	...	0.1	0.2	0.1	0.0	0.0	0.0
13	316	155	161	...	...	...	...	...	...	0.5	0.5	0.5	0.1	0.1	0.1
14	6479	3517	2962	...	...	...	...	...	...	9.5	10.2	8.8	1.6	1.6	1.6
15	7992	4599	3393	...	...	...	...	...	...	11.8	13.4	10.1	2.1	2.1	1.9
16	57406	30072	27334	...	...	...	...	...	...	84.6	87.5	81.5	14.2	13.6	14.9
17	17755	12804	4951	...	...	...	...	...	...	26.2	37.3	14.8	4.4	5.8	2.7
18	0	0	0	...	...	...	...	...	...	0.0	0.0	0.0	0.0	0.0	0.0
المجموع Total	404699	221375	183324	...	...	...	...	...	...	596.2	644.2	546.9	100.0	100.0	100.0
حجم السكان Population Size [II]	67885000	34364000	33521000							100000	100000	100000			

[1] Causes of death given in annex 1 — أسباب الوفاة في الملحق رقم 1
[II] World Population Prospects - 2000 Revision. — آفاق سكان العالم – مراجعة عام 2000.

جدول 16 (تابع) : أسباب الوفيات المسجلة : المعدل الخام والنسبة في المئة

Table 16 (cont'd): Registered Deaths by Cause: Crude Rates and Per Cent

الكويت KUWAIT 2005

سبب الوفاة cause of death [I]	المجموع العام Grand Total			المواطنون Nationals			غير مواطنين Non-Nationals			المعدل الخام (لكل مائة ألف من السكان) Rate (per 100 thousand population)			النسبة في المئة percent		
	مجموع Total	رجال Men	نساء Women	مجموع Total	رجال Men	نساء Women	مجموع Total	رجال Men	نساء Women	مجموع Total	رجال Men	نساء Women	مجموع Total	رجال Men	نساء Women
1	126	74	52	61	36	25	65	38	27	4.7	4.6	4.8	2.6	2.4	3.2
2	578	315	263	334	160	174	244	155	89	21.5	19.5	24.5	12.1	10.0	16.0
3	205	118	87	123	67	56	82	51	31	7.6	7.3	8.1	4.3	3.8	5.3
4	17	9	8	11	5	6	6	4	2	0.6	0.6	0.7	0.4	0.3	0.5
5	5	3	2	4	2	2	1	1	0	0.2	0.2	0.2	0.1	0.1	0.1
6	62	41	21	40	25	15	22	16	6	2.3	2.5	2.0	1.3	1.3	1.3
7	1952	1336	616	944	569	375	1008	767	241	72.6	82.9	57.3	40.8	42.6	37.4
8	244	129	115	162	86	76	82	43	39	9.1	8.0	10.7	5.1	4.1	7.0
9	136	76	60	72	33	39	64	43	21	5.1	4.7	5.6	2.8	2.4	3.6
10	82	48	34	60	35	25	22	13	9	3.1	3.0	3.2	1.7	1.5	2.1
11	2	0	2	1	0	1	1	0	1	0.1	0.0	0.2	0.0	0.0	0.1
12	10	3	7	6	2	4	4	1	3	0.4	0.2	0.7	0.2	0.1	0.4
13	3	2	1	0	0	0	3	2	1	0.1	0.1	0.1	0.1	0.1	0.1
14	240	130	110	133	69	64	107	61	46	8.9	8.1	10.2	5.0	4.1	6.7
15	167	87	80	100	57	43	67	30	37	6.2	5.4	7.4	3.5	2.8	4.9
16	123	61	62	89	43	46	34	18	16	4.6	3.8	5.8	2.6	1.9	3.8
17	...	...	...	0	0	0	0	0	0	...	...	...			
18	0	0	0	0	0	0	0	0	0	0.0	0.0	0.0	0.0	0.0	0.0
19	0	0	0	0	0	0	0	0	0	0.0	0.0	0.0	0.0	0.0	0.0
20	0	0	0	0	0	0	0	0	0	0.0	0.0	0.0	0.0	0.0	0.0
21	832	705	127	294	241	53	538	464	74	31.0	43.7	11.8	17.4	22.5	7.7
22	...	...	...	...	...	...	...	...	...	...	...	...	...	...	...
المجموع Total	4784	3137	1647	2434	1430	1004	2350	1707	643	178.0	194.6	153.2	100.0	100.0	1000.0
حجم السكان Population Size [II]	2687000	1612000	1075000							100000	100000	100000			

[I] Causes of death given in annex I   أسباب الوفيات في الملحق رقم 1

[II] "World Population Prospects - 2004 Revision.   آفاق سكان العالم – مراجعة عام 2004.

-47-

جدول 16 (تابع): أسباب الوفيات المسجلة : المعدل الخام والنسبة في المئة

Table 16 (cont'd): Registered Deaths by Cause: Crude Rates and Per Cent

KUWAIT 2004 — الكويت

cause of death [I]	Grand Total المجموع العام			Nationals المواطنون			Non-Nationals غير مواطنين			Rate (per 100 thousand population) المعدل الخام (لكل مائة ألف من السكان)			percent النسبة في المئة		
سبب الوفاة	Total مجموع	Men رجال	Women نساء	Total مجموع	Men رجال	Women نساء	Total مجموع	Men رجال	Women نساء	Total مجموع	Men رجال	Women نساء	Total مجموع	Men رجال	Women نساء
1	119	73	46	62	41	21	57	32	25	4.6	4.7	4.4	2.5	2.4	2.7
2	552	309	243	354	197	157	198	112	86	21.2	19.7	23.4	11.5	10.0	14.3
3	235	122	113	148	78	70	87	44	43	9.0	7.8	10.9	4.9	4.0	6.6
4	26	11	15	16	8	8	10	3	7	1.0	0.7	1.4	0.5	0.4	0.9
5	11	4	7	5	3	2	6	1	5	0.4	0.3	0.7	0.2	0.1	0.4
6	93	51	42	60	35	25	33	16	17	3.6	3.3	4.1	1.9	1.7	2.5
7	1928	1271	657	1043	616	427	885	655	230	74.0	81.0	63.4	40.2	41.2	38.5
8	214	115	99	119	69	50	95	46	49	8.2	7.3	9.5	4.5	3.7	5.8
9	124	81	43	51	28	23	73	53	20	4.8	5.2	4.1	2.6	2.6	2.5
10	69	30	39	53	27	26	16	3	13	2.6	1.9	3.8	1.4	1.0	2.3
11	6	0	6	3	0	3	3	0	3	0.2	0.0	0.6	0.1	0.0	0.4
12	7	0	7	5	0	5	2	0	2	0.3	0.0	0.7	0.1	0.0	0.4
13	5	2	3	2	0	2	3	2	1	0.2	0.1	0.3	0.1	0.1	0.2
14	249	127	122	153	83	70	96	44	52	9.6	8.1	11.8	5.2	4.1	7.2
15	167	102	65	100	58	42	67	44	23	6.4	6.5	6.3	3.5	3.3	3.8
16	91	36	55	56	26	30	35	10	25	3.5	2.3	5.3	1.9	1.2	3.2
17	897	754	143	443	383	60	454	371	83	34.4	48.1	13.8	18.7	24.4	8.4
18	0	0	0	0	0	0	0	0	0	0.0	0.0	0.0	0.0	0.0	0.0
Total المجموع	4793	3088	1705	2673	1652	1021	2120	1436	684	183.9	196.8	164.4	100.0	100.0	100.0
Population Size [II] حجم السكان	2606000	1569000	1037000							100000	100000	100000			

[I] Causes of death given in annex 1

[II] "World Population Prospects - 2004 Revision.

1 أسباب الوفيات في الملحق رقم 1

"آفاق سكان العالم – مراجعة عام 2004."

الكويت KUWAIT

جدول 16 (تابع): أسباب الوفيات المسجلة : المعدل الخام والنسبة في المئة

Table 16 (cont'd): Registered Deaths by Cause: Crude Rates and Per Cent

سبب الوفاة cause of death [1]	المجموع العام Grand Total مجموع Total	رجال Men	نساء Women	المواطنين Nationals مجموع Total	رجال Men	نساء Women	غير مواطنين Non-Nationals مجموع Total	رجال Men	نساء Women	المعدل الخام (لكل مائة ألف من السكان) Rate (per 100 thousand population) مجموع Total	رجال Men	نساء Women	النسبة في المئة percent مجموع Total	رجال Men	نساء Women
1	104	56	48	47	26	21	57	30	27	4.1	3.7	4.8	2.4	2.0	3.0
2	537	273	264	324	160	164	213	113	100	21.3	18.0	26.3	12.1	9.7	16.5
3	248	123	125	165	83	82	83	40	43	9.8	8.1	12.5	5.6	4.4	7.8
4	24	8	16	11	4	7	13	4	9	1.0	0.5	1.6	0.5	0.3	1.0
5	9	6	3	3	2	1	6	4	2	0.4	0.4	0.3	0.2	0.2	0.2
6	62	42	20	32	24	8	30	18	12	2.5	2.8	2.0	1.4	1.5	1.2
7	1814	1211	603	993	597	396	821	614	207	72.0	79.8	60.1	41.0	42.9	37.6
8	233	132	101	153	95	58	80	37	43	9.2	8.7	10.1	5.3	4.7	6.3
9	88	64	24	44	32	12	44	32	12	3.5	4.2	2.4	2.0	2.3	1.5
10	63	34	29	46	25	21	17	9	8	2.5	2.2	2.9	1.4	1.2	1.8
11	4	0	4	1	0	1	3	0	3	0.2	0.0	0.4	0.1	0.0	0.2
12	0	0	0	0	0	0	0	0	0	0.0	0.0	0.0	0.0	0.0	0.0
13	0	0	0	0	0	0	0	0	0	0.0	0.0	0.0	0.0	0.0	0.0
14	231	121	110	131	68	63	100	53	47	9.2	8.0	11.0	5.2	4.3	6.9
15	160	87	73	92	49	43	68	38	30	6.3	5.7	7.3	3.6	3.1	4.6
16	119	53	66	78	38	40	41	15	26	4.7	3.5	6.6	2.7	1.9	4.1
17	728	612	116	332	287	45	396	325	71	28.9	40.3	11.6	16.5	21.7	7.2
18	0	0	0	0	0	0	0	0	0	0.0	0.0	0.0	0.0	0.0	0.0
المجموع Total	4424	2822	1602	2452	1490	962	1972	1332	640	175.5	185.9	159.7	100.0	100.0	100.0
حجم السكان Population Size [II]	2521000	1518000	1003000							100000	100000	100000			

[1] Causes of death given in annex 1

[II] World Population Prospects - 2002 Revision.

1 أسباب الوفيات في الملحق رقم 1

II آفاق سكان العالم - مراجعة عام 2002.

الكويت KUWAIT 2002

سبب الوفاة cause of death [1]	المجموع العام Grand Total			المواطنون Nationals			غير مواطنين Non-Nationals			المعدل الخام (لكل مائة ألف من السكان) Rate (per 100 thousand population)			النسبة في المئة percent		
	مجموع Total	رجال Men	نساء Women	مجموع Total	رجال Men	نساء Women	مجموع Total	رجال Men	نساء Women	مجموع Total	رجال Men	نساء Women	مجموع Total	رجال Men	نساء Women
1	117	76	41	56	36	20	61	40	21	4.8	5.2	4.2	2.7	2.8	2.6
2	552	290	262	238	133	105	314	157	157	22.6	19.7	27.0	12.7	10.5	16.5
3	260	146	114	91	54	37	169	92	77	10.6	9.9	11.8	6.0	5.3	7.2
4	22	10	12	13	8	5	9	2	7	0.9	0.7	1.2	0.5	0.4	0.8
5	9	4	5	0	0	0	9	4	5	0.4	0.3	0.5	0.2	0.1	0.3
6	79	43	36	25	15	10	54	28	26	3.2	2.9	3.7	1.8	1.6	2.3
7	1713	1147	566	799	591	208	914	556	358	70.1	77.9	58.4	39.5	41.6	35.7
8	221	127	94	70	38	32	151	89	62	9.0	8.6	9.7	5.1	4.6	5.9
9	111	67	44	43	30	13	68	37	31	4.5	4.5	4.5	2.6	2.4	2.8
10	72	43	29	26	15	11	46	28	18	2.9	2.9	3.0	1.7	1.6	1.8
11	3	0	3	1	0	1	2	0	2	0.1	0.0	0.3	0.1	0.0	0.2
12	7	2	5	3	1	2	4	1	3	0.3	0.1	0.5	0.2	0.1	0.3
13	2	2	0	0	0	0	2	2	0	0.1	0.1	0.0	0.0	0.1	0.0
14	231	127	104	76	50	26	155	77	78	9.5	8.6	10.7	5.3	4.6	6.6
15	173	90	83	62	31	31	111	59	52	7.1	6.1	8.6	4.0	3.3	5.2
16	126	55	71	46	14	32	80	41	39	5.2	3.7	7.3	2.9	2.0	4.5
17	644	526	118	382	316	66	262	210	52	26.4	35.7	12.2	14.8	19.1	7.4
18	0	0	0	0	0	0	0	0	0	0.0	0.0	0.0	0.0	0.0	0.0
المجموع Total	4342	2755	1587	1931	1332	599	2411	1423	988	177.7	187.0	163.6	100.0	100.0	100.0
حجم السكان Population Size [II]	2443000	1473000	970000							100000	100000	100000			

-50-

[1] Causes of death given in annex 1   أسباب الوفيات في الملحق رقم 1

[II] "World Population Prospects - 2002 Revision."   "آفاق سكان العالم - مراجعة عام 2002."

جدول 16 (تابع) : أسباب الوفيات المسجلة : المعدل الخام والنسبة في المئة

Table 16 (cont'd): Registered Deaths by Cause: Crude Rates and Per Cent

الكويت KUWAIT
2001

سبب الوفاة cause of death	المجموع العام Grand Total			المواطنون Nationals			غير مواطنين Non-Nationals			المعدل الخام (لكل مائة ألف من السكان) Rate (per 100 thousand population)			النسبة في المئة percent		
	مجموع Total	رجال Men	نساء Women	مجموع Total	رجال Men	نساء Women	مجموع Total	رجال Men	نساء Women	مجموع Total	رجال Men	نساء Women	مجموع Total	رجال Men	نساء Women
1	92	51	41	43	23	20	49	28	21	4.7	4.5	5.0	2.1	1.8	2.6
2	531	270	261	190	106	84	341	164	177	26.9	23.6	31.6	12.2	9.8	16.3
3	255	137	118	89	49	40	166	88	78	12.9	12.0	14.3	5.8	5.0	7.4
4	23	11	12	4	3	1	19	8	11	1.2	1.0	1.5	0.5	0.4	0.7
5	5	5	0	2	2	0	3	3	0	0.3	0.4	0.0	0.1	0.2	0.0
6	73	53	20	37	31	6	36	22	14	3.7	4.6	2.4	1.7	1.9	1.2
7	1753	1150	603	815	606	209	938	544	394	88.9	100.4	73.0	40.2	41.7	37.6
8	217	136	81	89	56	33	128	80	48	11.0	11.9	9.8	5.0	4.9	5.1
9	110	67	43	55	36	19	55	31	24	5.6	5.9	5.2	2.5	2.4	2.7
10	60	31	29	22	8	14	38	23	15	3.0	2.7	3.5	1.4	1.1	1.8
11	1	0	1	1	0	1	0	0	0	0.1	0.0	0.1	0.0	0.0	0.1
12	3	0	3	2	0	2	1	0	1	0.2	0.0	0.4	0.1	0.0	0.2
13	4	0	4	2	0	2	2	0	2	0.2	0.0	0.5	0.1	0.0	0.2
14	239	126	113	86	38	48	153	88	65	12.1	11.0	13.7	5.5	4.6	7.0
15	164	97	67	67	47	20	97	50	47	8.3	8.5	8.1	3.8	3.5	4.2
16	176	91	85	64	34	30	112	57	55	8.9	7.9	10.3	4.0	3.3	5.3
17	658	536	122	351	282	69	307	254	53	33.4	46.8	14.8	15.1	19.4	7.6
18	0	0	0	0	0	0	0	0	0	0.0	0.0	0.0	0.0	0.0	0.0
المجموع Total	4364	2761	1603	1919	1321	598	2445	1440	1005	221.4	241.1	194.1	100.0	100.0	100.0
حجم السكان Population Size II	1971000	1145000	826000				100000	100000	100000	100000	100000	100000			

I Causes of death given in annex 1
أسباب الوفيات في الملحق رقم 1

II World Population Prospects - 2000 Revision.
آفاق سكان العالم - مراجعة عام 2000.

جدول 16 (تابع) (تابع) 16

Table 16 (cont'd): Registered Deaths by Cause: Crude Rates and Per Cent

المعدل الخام والنسبة في المئة : أسباب الوفيات المسجلة

cause of death [I] سبب الوفاة	المجموع العام Grand Total المجموع ع العام			المواطنون Nationals			غير مواطنين Non-Nationals			المعدل الخام (لكل مائة ألف من السكان) Rate (per 100 thousand population)			النسبة في المئة percent		
	مجموع Total	رجال Men	نساء Women	مجموع Total	رجال Men	نساء Women	مجموع Total	رجال Men	نساء Women	مجموع Total	رجال Men	نساء Women	مجموع Total	رجال Men	نساء Wcmen
1	98	63	35	51	32	19	47	31	16	5.1	5.7	4.4	2.3	2.3	2.3
2	519	269	250	323	166	157	196	103	93	27.1	24.1	31.3	12.3	10.0	16.3
3	243	132	111	187	102	85	56	30	26	12.7	11.8	13.9	5.7	4.9	7.2
4	20	14	6	16	12	4	4	2	2	1.0	1.3	0.8	0.5	0.5	0.4
5	11	9	2	8	6	2	3	3	0	0.6	0.8	0.3	0.3	0.3	0.1
6	73	49	24	39	27	12	34	22	12	3.8	4.4	3.0	1.7	1.8	1.6
7	1695	1133	562	914	541	373	781	592	189	88.5	101.6	70.3	40.1	42.1	36.6
8	203	104	99	132	70	62	71	34	37	10.6	9.3	12.4	4.8	3.9	6.4
9	103	69	34	59	38	21	44	31	13	5.4	6.2	4.3	2.4	2.6	2.2
10	86	49	37	66	38	28	20	11	9	4.5	4.4	4.6	2.0	1.8	2.4
11	4	0	4	0	0	0	4	0	4	0.2	0.0	0.5	0.1	0.0	0.3
12	4	1	3	3	1	2	1	0	1	0.2	0.1	0.4	0.1	0.0	0.2
13	1	1	0	1	1	0	0	0	0	0.1	0.1	0.0	0.0	0.0	0.0
14	201	108	93	126	68	58	75	40	35	10.5	9.7	11.6	4.8	4.0	6.1
15	160	99	61	98	59	39	62	40	22	8.4	8.9	7.6	3.8	3.7	4.0
16	147	69	78	103	53	50	44	16	28	7.7	6.2	9.8	3.5	2.6	5.1
17	659	521	138	294	234	60	365	287	78	34.4	46.7	17.3	15.6	19.4	9.0
18	0	0	0	0	0	0	0	0	0	0.0	0.0	0.0	0.0	0.0	0.0
المجموع Total	4227	2690	1537	2420	1448	972	1807	1242	565	220.7	241.3	192.1	100.0	100.0	100.0
حجم السكان [II] Population Size	1915000	1115000	800000							100000	100000	100000			

الكويت KUWAIT 2000

-52-

[I] Causes of death given in annex 1 — أسباب الوفيات في الملحق رقم 1

[II] "World Population Prospects - 2000 Revision." — "آفاق سكان العالم – مراجعة عام 2000."

الكويت KUWAIT 2003

cause of death سبب الوفاة	المجموع العام Grand Total			المواطنون Nationals			غير مواطنين Non-Nationals			المعدل الخام Rate (per 100 thousand population)			النسبة في المئة percent		
	مجموع Total	رجال Men	نساء Women	مجموع Total	رجال Men	نساء Women	مجموع Total	رجال Men	نساء Women	مجموع Total	رجال Men	نساء Women	مجموع Total	رجال Men	نساء Women
1	104	56	48	47	26	21	57	30	27	4.1	3.7	4.8	2.4	2.0	3.0
2	537	273	264	324	160	164	213	113	100	21.3	18.0	26.3	12.1	9.7	16.5
3	248	123	125	165	83	82	83	40	43	9.8	8.1	12.5	5.6	4.4	7.8
4	24	8	16	11	4	7	13	4	9	1.0	0.5	1.6	0.5	0.3	1.0
5	9	6	3	3	2	1	6	4	2	0.4	0.4	0.3	0.2	0.2	0.2
6	62	42	20	32	24	8	30	18	12	2.5	2.8	2.0	1.4	1.5	1.2
7	1814	1211	603	993	597	396	821	614	207	72.0	79.8	60.1	41.0	42.9	37.6
8	233	132	101	153	95	58	80	37	43	9.2	8.7	10.1	5.3	4.7	6.3
9	88	64	24	44	32	12	44	32	12	3.5	4.2	2.4	2.0	2.3	1.5
10	63	34	29	46	25	21	17	9	8	2.5	2.2	2.9	1.4	1.2	1.8
11	4	0	4	1	0	1	3	0	3	0.2	0.0	0.4	0.1	0.0	0.2
12	0	0	0	0	0	0	0	0	0	0.0	0.0	0.0	0.0	0.0	0.0
13	0	0	0	0	0	0	0	0	0	0.0	0.0	0.0	0.0	0.0	0.0
14	231	121	110	131	68	63	100	53	47	9.2	8.0	11.0	5.2	4.3	6.9
15	160	87	73	92	49	43	68	38	30	6.3	5.7	7.3	3.6	3.1	4.6
16	119	53	66	78	38	40	41	15	26	4.7	3.5	6.6	2.7	1.9	4.1
17	728	612	116	332	287	45	396	325	71	28.9	40.3	11.6	16.5	21.7	7.2
18	0	0	0	0	0	0	0	0	0	0.0	0.0	0.0	0.0	0.0	0.0
المجموع Total	4424	2822	1602	2452	1490	962	1972	1332	640	175.5	185.9	159.7	100.0	100.0	100.0
حجم السكان Population Size [II]	2521000	1518000	1003000	100000	100000	100000				100000					

[I] Causes of death given in annex 1   أسباب الوفيات في الملحق رقم 1

[II] World Population Prospects - 2002 Revision.   آفاق سكان العالم – مراجعة عام 2002.

جدول 16 (تابع) : أسباب الوفيات المسجلة : المعدل الخام والنسبة في المئة

Table 16 (cont'd): Registered Deaths by Cause: Crude Rates and Per Cent

KUWAIT 2002 / cause of death [1]	Grand Total			Nationals			Non-Nationals			Rate (per 100 thousand population)			percent		
	Total	Men	Women	Total	Men	Women	Total	Men	Women	Total	Men	Women	Total	Men	Women
1	117	76	41	56	36	20	61	40	21	4.8	5.2	4.2	2.7	2.8	2.6
2	552	290	262	238	133	105	314	157	157	22.6	19.7	27.0	12.7	10.5	16.5
3	260	146	114	91	54	37	169	92	77	10.6	9.9	11.8	6.0	5.3	7.2
4	22	10	12	13	8	5	9	2	7	0.9	0.7	1.2	0.5	0.4	0.8
5	9	4	5	0	0	0	9	4	5	0.4	0.3	0.5	0.2	0.1	0.3
6	79	43	36	25	15	10	54	28	26	3.2	2.9	3.7	1.8	1.6	2.3
7	1713	1147	566	799	591	208	914	556	358	70.1	77.9	58.4	39.5	41.6	35.7
8	221	127	94	70	38	32	151	89	62	9.0	8.6	9.7	5.1	4.6	5.9
9	111	67	44	43	30	13	68	37	31	4.5	4.5	4.5	2.6	2.4	2.8
10	72	43	29	26	15	11	46	28	18	2.9	2.9	3.0	1.7	1.6	1.8
11	3	0	3	1	0	1	2	0	2	0.1	0.0	0.3	0.1	0.0	0.2
12	7	2	5	3	1	2	4	1	3	0.3	0.1	0.5	0.2	0.1	0.3
13	2	2	0	0	0	0	2	2	0	0.1	0.1	0.0	0.0	0.1	0.0
14	231	127	104	76	50	26	155	77	78	9.5	8.6	10.7	5.3	4.6	6.6
15	173	90	83	62	31	31	111	59	52	7.1	6.1	8.6	4.0	3.3	5.2
16	126	55	71	46	14	32	80	41	39	5.2	3.7	7.3	2.9	2.0	4.5
17	644	526	118	382	316	66	262	210	52	26.4	35.7	12.2	14.8	19.1	7.4
18	0	0	0	0	0	0	0	0	0	0.0	0.0	0.0	0.0	0.0	0.0
Total	4342	2755	1587	1931	1332	599	2411	1423	988	177.7	187.0	163.6	100.0	100.0	100.0
Population Size [2]	2443000	1473000	970000							100000	100000	100000			

[1] Causes of death given in annex 1
[2] "World Population Prospects - 2002 Revision."

¹ أسباب الوفيات في الملحق رقم 1
² «آفاق سكان العالم – مراجعة عام 2002».

جدول 16 (تابع): المعدل الخام والنسبة في المئة : أسباب الوفيات المسجلة
Table 16 (cont'd): Registered Deaths by Cause: Crude Rates and Per Cent

عمان* OMAN*
2006

سبب الوفاة cause of death [I]	المجموع العام Grand Total			المواطنون Nationals			غير مواطنين Non-Nationals			المعدل الخام (لكل مائة ألف من السكان) Rate (per 100 thousand population)			النسبة في المئة percent		
	مجموع Total	رجال Men	نساء Women	مجموع Total	رجال Men	نساء Women	مجموع Total	رجال Men	نساء Women	مجموع Total	رجال Men	نساء Women	مجموع Total	رجال Men	نساء Women
1	584	329	255	…	…	…	…	…	…	31.0	34.6	27.4	19.3	18.3	20.7
2	282	160	122	…	…	…	…	…	…	15.0	16.8	13.1	9.3	8.9	9.9
3	47	18	29	…	…	…	…	…	…	2.5	1.9	3.1	1.6	1.0	2.4
4	17	11	6	…	…	…	…	…	…	0.9	1.2	0.6	0.6	0.6	0.5
5	4	4	0	…	…	…	…	…	…	0.2	0.4	0.0	0.1	0.2	0.0
6	78	51	27	…	…	…	…	…	…	4.1	5.4	2.9	2.6	2.8	2.2
7	847	471	376	…	…	…	…	…	…	45.0	49.5	40.3	28.0	26.2	30.5
8	244	152	92	…	…	…	…	…	…	13.0	16.0	9.9	8.1	8.5	7.5
9	113	80	33	…	…	…	…	…	…	6.0	8.4	3.5	3.7	4.5	2.7
10	65	40	25	…	…	…	…	…	…	3.5	4.2	2.7	2.1	2.2	2.0
11	3	0	3	…	…	…	…	…	…	0.2	0.0	0.3	0.1	0.0	0.2
12	3	1	2	…	…	…	…	…	…	0.2	0.1	0.2	0.1	0.1	0.2
13	9	4	5	…	…	…	…	…	…	0.5	0.4	0.5	0.3	0.2	0.4
14	85	49	36	…	…	…	…	…	…	4.5	5.2	3.9	2.8	2.7	2.9
15	167	103	64	…	…	…	…	…	…	8.9	10.8	6.9	5.5	5.7	5.2
16	173	99	74	…	…	…	…	…	…	9.2	10.4	7.9	5.7	5.5	6.0
17	207	162	45	…	…	…	…	…	…	11.0	17.0	4.8	6.8	9.0	3.7
18	96	59	37	…	…	…	…	…	…	5.1	6.2	4.0	3.2	3.3	3.0
19	0	0	0	…	…	…	…	…	…	0.0	0.0	0.0	0.0	0.0	0.0
20	0	0	0	…	…	…	…	…	…	0.0	0.0	0.0	0.0	0.0	0.0
21	0	0	0	…	…	…	…	…	…	0.0	0.0	0.0	0.0	0.0	0.0
22	3	2	1	…	…	…	…	…	…	0.2	0.2	0.1	0.1	0.1	0.1
المجموع Total	3027	1795	1232	…	…	…	…	…	…	160.7	188.7	132.2	100.0	100.0	100.0
حجم السكان Population Size [II]	1883576	951440	932136							100000.0	100000.0	100000.0			

[I] Causes of death given in annex 1   أسباب الوفيات في الملحق رقم 1
[II] National population estimates   تقديرات السكان
* Causes of deaths are for the deads in the hospital   الوفيات حسب السبب للمتوفين في المستشفيات

-53-

عمان* OMAN*

جدول 16 (تابع) : أسباب الوفيات المسجلة : المعدل الخام والنسبة في المئة

Table 16 (cont'd): Registered Deaths by Cause: Crude Rates and Per Cent

cause of death [I] سبب الوفاة	Grand Total المجموع العام Total مجموع	Men رجال	Women نساء	Nationals المواطنون Total مجموع	Men رجال	Women نساء	Non-Nationals غير مواطنين Total مجموع	Men رجال	Women نساء	Rate (per 100 thousand population) المعدل الخام (لكل مائة ألف من السكان) Total مجموع	Men رجال	Women نساء	percent النسبة في المئة Total مجموع	Men رجال	Women نساء
1	521	301	220	...	...	...	...	...	...	28.3	32.3	24.1	18.3	13.1	18.5
2	269	159	110	...	...	...	...	...	...	14.6	17.1	12.1	9.4	9.6	9.3
3	79	44	35	...	...	...	...	...	...	4.3	4.7	3.8	2.8	2.6	3.0
4	27	20	7	...	...	...	...	...	...	1.5	2.1	0.8	0.9	1.2	0.6
5	4	3	1	...	...	...	...	...	...	0.2	0.3	0.1	0.1	0.2	0.1
6	72	46	26	...	...	...	...	...	...	3.9	4.9	2.9	2.5	2.8	2.2
7	876	491	385	...	...	...	...	...	...	47.5	52.7	42.2	30.7	29.5	32.5
8	205	110	95	...	...	...	...	...	...	11.1	11.8	10.4	7.2	6.6	8.0
9	124	80	44	...	...	...	...	...	...	6.7	8.6	4.8	4.4	4.8	3.7
10	55	36	19	...	...	...	...	...	...	3.0	3.9	2.1	1.9	2.2	1.6
11	6	0	6	...	...	...	...	...	...	0.3	0.0	0.7	0.2	0.0	0.5
12	11	7	4	...	...	...	...	...	...	0.6	0.8	0.4	0.4	0.4	0.3
13	3	1	2	...	...	...	...	...	...	0.2	0.1	0.2	0.1	0.1	0.2
14	102	51	51	...	...	...	...	...	...	5.5	5.5	5.6	3.6	3.1	4.3
15	150	86	64	...	...	...	...	...	...	8.1	9.2	7.0	5.3	5.2	5.4
16	129	68	61	...	...	...	...	...	...	7.0	7.3	6.7	4.5	4.1	5.1
17	212	158	54	...	...	...	...	...	...	11.5	17.0	5.9	7.4	9.5	4.6
18	0	0	0	...	...	...	...	...	...	0.0	0.0	0.0	0.0	0.0	0.0
19	0	0	0	...	...	...	...	...	...	0.0	0.0	0.0	0.0	0.0	0.0
20	0	0	0	...	...	...	...	...	...	0.0	0.0	0.0	0.0	0.0	0.0
21	0	0	0	...	...	...	...	...	...	0.0	0.0	0.0	0.0	0.0	0.0
22	4	2	2	...	...	...	...	...	...	0.2	0.2	0.2	0.1	0.1	0.2
المجموع Total	2849	1663	1186	...	...	...	...	...	...	154.6	178.6	130.1	100.0	100.0	100.0
حجم السكان Population Size [II]	1842684	931007	911677							100000.0	100000.0	100000.0			

2005

[I] أسباب الوفيات في الملحق رقم 1
[II] تقديرات السكان
* الوفيات حسب السبب الرئيسي للمتوفين في المستشفيات

[I] Causes of death given in annex 1
[II] National population estimates
* Causes of deaths are for the deads in the hospital

-54-

جدول 16 (تابع): أسباب الوفيات المسجلة : المعدل الخام والنسبة في المئة

Table 16 (cont'd): Registered Deaths by Cause: Crude Rates and Per Cent

عمان OMAN*
2004

سبب الوفاة cause of death	المجموع العام Grand Total مجموع Total	رجال Men	نساء Women	المواطنون Nationals مجموع Total	رجال Men	نساء Women	غير مواطنين Non-Nationals مجموع Total	رجال Men	نساء Women	المعدل الخام (لكل مائة ألف من السكان) Rate (per 100 thousand population) مجموع Total	رجال Men	نساء Women	النسبة في المئة percent مجموع Total	رجال Men	نساء Women
1	436	258	178	...	...	...	...	...	...	18.0	19.0	16.9	15.9	15.6	16.3
2	259	146	113	...	...	...	...	...	...	10.7	10.7	10.7	9.4	8.8	10.3
3	63	38	25	...	...	...	...	...	...	2.6	2.8	2.4	2.3	2.3	2.3
4	26	17	9	...	...	...	...	...	...	1.1	1.2	0.9	0.9	1.0	0.8
5	5	1	4	...	...	...	...	...	...	0.2	0.1	0.4	0.2	0.1	0.4
6	64	47	17	...	...	...	...	...	...	2.6	3.5	1.6	2.3	2.8	1.6
7	922	551	371	...	...	...	...	...	...	38.2	40.5	35.2	33.6	33.4	34.0
8	207	118	89	...	...	...	...	...	...	8.6	8.7	8.4	7.5	7.1	8.2
9	92	50	42	...	...	...	...	...	...	3.8	3.7	4.0	3.4	3.0	3.8
10	61	38	23	...	...	...	...	...	...	2.5	2.8	2.2	2.2	2.3	2.1
11	3	0	3	...	...	...	...	...	...	0.1	0.0	0.3	0.1	0.0	0.3
12	7	5	2	...	...	...	...	...	...	0.3	0.4	0.2	0.3	0.3	0.2
13	14	5	9	...	...	...	...	...	...	0.6	0.4	0.9	0.5	0.3	0.8
14	112	56	56	...	...	...	...	...	...	4.6	4.1	5.3	4.1	3.4	5.1
15	147	90	57	...	...	...	...	...	...	6.1	6.6	5.4	5.4	5.5	5.2
16	119	75	44	...	...	...	...	...	...	4.9	5.5	4.2	4.3	4.5	4.0
17	197	153	44	...	...	...	...	...	...	8.2	11.2	4.2	7.2	9.3	4.0
18	9	3	6	...	...	...	...	...	...	0.4	0.2	0.6	0.3	0.2	0.5
19	...	...	...	...	...	...	...	...	...	...	...	...	...	...	...
20	...	...	...	...	...	...	...	...	...	...	...	...	...	...	...
21	...	...	...	...	...	...	...	...	...	...	...	...	...	...	...
22	...	...	...	...	...	...	...	...	...	...	...	...	...	...	...
المجموع Total	2743	1651	1092	...	...	...	...	...	...	113.6	121.3	103.5	100.0	100.0	100.0
حجم السكان Population Size II	2415576	1360891	1054685							100000.0	100000.0	100000.0			

I Causes of death given in annex 1
أسباب الوفيات في الملحق رقم 1 I

II National population estimates
تقديرات السكان: مصادر وطنية II

* Causes of deaths are for the deads in the hospital
الوفيات حسب السبب للمتوفين في المستشفيات *

جدول 16 (تابع): أسباب الوفيات المسجلة : المعدل الخام والنسبة في المئة

Table 16 (cont'd): Registered Deaths by Cause: Crude Rates and Per Cent

OMAN* عمان*

2003

cause of death [I] سبب الوفاة	Grand Total المجموع العام			Nationals المواطنون			Non-Nationals غير مواطنين			Rate (per 100 thousand population) المعدل الخام (لكل مائة ألف من السكان)			percent النسبة في المئة		
	Total مجموع	Men رجال	Women نساء	Total مجموع	Men رجال	Women نساء	Total مجموع	Men رجال	Women نساء	Total مجموع	Men رجال	Women نساء	Total مجموع	Men رجال	Women نساء
1	397	224	173	...	...	...	...	...	...	17.0	17.1	16.8	14.7	14.1	15.5
2	253	150	103	...	...	...	...	...	...	10.8	11.4	10.0	9.4	9.5	9.2
3	62	30	32	...	...	...	...	...	...	2.6	2.3	3.1	2.3	1.9	2.9
4	27	15	12	...	...	...	...	...	...	1.2	1.1	1.2	1.0	0.9	1.1
5	5	4	1	...	...	...	...	...	...	0.2	0.3	0.1	0.2	0.3	0.1
6	56	36	20	...	...	...	...	...	...	2.4	2.7	1.9	2.1	2.3	1.8
7	883	495	388	...	...	...	...	...	...	37.7	37.7	37.8	32.7	31.2	34.8
8	251	137	114	...	...	...	...	...	...	10.7	10.4	11.1	9.3	8.6	10.2
9	102	68	34	...	...	...	...	...	...	4.4	5.2	3.3	3.8	4.3	3.1
10	73	41	32	...	...	...	...	...	...	3.1	3.1	3.1	2.7	2.6	2.9
11	2	0	2	...	...	...	...	...	...	0.1	0.0	0.2	0.1	0.0	0.2
12	9	6	3	...	...	...	...	...	...	0.4	0.5	0.3	0.3	0.4	0.3
13	6	3	3	...	...	...	...	...	...	0.3	0.2	0.3	0.2	0.2	0.3
14	115	61	54	...	...	...	...	...	...	4.9	4.6	5.3	4.3	3.8	4.8
15	149	92	57	...	...	...	...	...	...	6.4	7.0	5.5	5.5	5.8	5.1
16	88	53	35	...	...	...	...	...	...	3.8	4.0	3.4	3.3	3.3	3.1
17	214	167	47	...	...	...	...	...	...	9.1	12.7	4.6	7.9	10.5	4.2
18	9	5	4	...	...	...	...	...	...	0.4	0.4	0.4	0.3	0.3	0.4
Total المجموع	2701	1587	1114	...	...	...	...	...	...	115.4	120.8	108.4	100.0	100.0	100.0
Population Size [II] حجم السكان	2340815	1313239	1027576							100000	100000	100000			

[I] Causes of death given in annex 1   أسباب الوفيات في الملحق رقم 1

[II] National population estimates   تقديرات السكان: مصادر وطنية

* Causes of deaths are for the deads in the hospital   الوفيات حسب السبب للمتوفين في المستشفيات

جدول 16 (تابع): أسباب الوفيات المسجلة : المعدل الخام والنسبة في المئة

Table 16 (cont'd): Registered Deaths by Cause: Crude Rates and Per Cent

عمان* OMAN*

2002

سبب الوفاة cause of death	المجموع العام Grand Total			المواطنين Nationals			غير مواطنين Non-Nationals			المعدل الخام (لكل مائة ألف من السكان) Rate (per 100 thousand population)			النسبة في المئة percent		
	مجموع Total	رجال Men	نساء Women	مجموع Total	رجال Men	نساء Women	مجموع Total	رجال Men	نساء Women	مجموع Total	رجال Men	نساء Women	مجموع Total	رجال Men	نساء Women
1	339	196	143	…	…	…	…	…	…	18.1	20.6	15.6	13.2	12.8	13.8
2	262	158	104	…	…	…	…	…	…	14.0	16.6	11.3	10.2	10.3	10.1
3	54	28	26	…	…	…	…	…	…	2.9	2.9	2.8	2.1	1.8	2.5
4	21	11	10	…	…	…	…	…	…	1.1	1.2	1.1	0.8	0.7	1.0
5	1	0	1	…	…	…	…	…	…	0.1	0.0	0.1	0.0	0.0	0.1
6	72	44	28	…	…	…	…	…	…	3.9	4.6	3.0	2.8	2.9	2.7
7	844	509	335	…	…	…	…	…	…	45.1	53.5	36.5	32.9	33.2	32.4
8	213	127	86	…	…	…	…	…	…	11.4	13.4	9.4	8.3	8.3	8.3
9	102	80	22	…	…	…	…	…	…	5.5	8.4	2.4	4.0	5.2	2.1
10	77	34	43	…	…	…	…	…	…	4.1	3.6	4.7	3.0	2.2	4.2
11	7	0	7	…	…	…	…	…	…	0.4	0.0	0.8	0.3	0.0	0.7
12	4	4	0	…	…	…	…	…	…	0.2	0.4	0.0	0.2	0.3	0.0
13	5	4	1	…	…	…	…	…	…	0.3	0.4	0.1	0.2	0.3	0.1
14	114	60	54	…	…	…	…	…	…	6.1	6.3	5.9	4.4	3.9	5.2
15	168	98	70	…	…	…	…	…	…	9.0	10.3	7.6	6.6	6.4	6.8
16	94	46	48	…	…	…	…	…	…	5.0	4.8	5.2	3.7	3.0	4.6
17	181	128	53	…	…	…	…	…	…	9.7	13.5	5.8	7.1	8.4	5.1
18	6	4	2	…	…	…	…	…	…	0.3	0.4	0.2	0.2	0.3	0.2
المجموع Total	2564	1531	1033	…	…	…	…	…	…	137.1	161.0	112.4	100.0	100.0	100.0
حجم السكان Population Size II	1869580	950666	918914										100000.0	100000.0	100000.0

I Causes of death given in annex 1
II National population estimates
* Causes of deaths are for the deads in the hospital

۱ أسباب الوفاة في الملحق رقم ۱
۱۱ تقدير السكان: مصادر وطنية
* الوفيات حسب السبب للمتوفين في المستشفيات

جدول 16 (تابع): أسباب الوفيات المسجلة : المعدل الخام والنسبة في المئة

Table 16 (cont'd): Registered Deaths by Cause: Crude Rates and Per Cent

OMAN* عمان* 2001	cause of death سبب الوفاة [1]	Grand Total المجموع العام			Nationals المواطنون			Non-Nationals غير مواطنين			Rate (per 100 thousand population) المعدل الخام (لكل مائة ألف من السكان)			percent النسبة في المئة		
		مجموع Total	رجال Men	نساء Women	مجموع Total	رجال Men	نساء Women	مجموع Total	رجال Men	نساء Women	مجموع Total	رجال Men	نساء Women	مجموع Total	رجال Men	نساء Women
	1	259	145	114	...	...	...	...	...	...	14.2	15.6	12.7	10.2	9.5	11.1
	2	274	167	107	...	...	...	...	...	...	15.0	18.0	11.9	10.7	10.9	10.5
	3	61	34	27	...	...	...	...	...	...	3.3	3.7	3.0	2.4	2.2	2.6
	4	22	15	7	...	...	...	...	...	...	1.2	1.6	0.8	0.9	1.0	0.7
	5	9	5	4	...	...	...	...	...	...	0.5	0.5	0.4	0.4	0.3	0.4
	6	54	28	26	...	...	...	...	...	...	3.0	3.0	2.9	2.1	1.8	2.5
	7	936	550	386	...	...	...	...	...	...	51.3	59.2	43.0	36.7	36.0	37.7
	8	229	128	101	...	...	...	...	...	...	12.5	13.8	11.3	9.0	8.4	9.9
	9	93	58	35	...	...	...	...	...	...	5.1	6.2	3.9	3.6	3.8	3.4
	10	58	38	20	...	...	...	...	...	...	3.2	4.1	2.2	2.3	2.5	2.0
	11	2	0	2	...	...	...	...	...	...	0.1	0.0	0.2	0.1	0.0	0.2
	12	9	3	6	...	...	...	...	...	...	0.5	0.3	0.7	0.4	0.2	0.6
	13	1	0	1	...	...	...	...	...	...	0.1	0.0	0.1	0.0	0.0	0.1
	14	102	65	37	...	...	...	...	...	...	5.6	7.0	4.1	4.0	4.3	3.6
	15	188	109	79	...	...	...	...	...	...	10.3	11.7	8.8	7.4	7.1	7.7
	16	78	46	32	...	...	...	...	...	...	4.3	5.0	3.6	3.1	3.0	3.1
	17	173	135	38	...	...	...	...	...	...	9.5	14.5	4.2	6.8	8.8	3.7
	18	2	1	1	...	...	...	...	...	...	0.1	0.1	0.1	0.1	0.1	0.1
المجموع Total		2550	1527	1023	...	...	...	...	...	...	139.6	164.4	114.0	100.0	100.0	100.0
حجم السكان Population Size [II]		1826124	928747	897377							100000	100000	100000			

[1] أسباب الوفيات في ملحق رقم 1 / Causes of death given in annex 1
[II] تقديرات السكان: مصدر، وظيفة / National population estimates
* الوفيات حسب السبب للمتوفين في المستشفيات / Causes of deaths are for the deads in the hospital

جدول 16 (تابع) : أسباب الوفيات المسجلة : المعدل الخام والنسبة في المئة
Table 16 (cont'd): Registered Deaths by Cause: Crude Rates and Per Cent

عمان* OMAN*
2000

سبب الوفاة ¹ cause of death	المجموع العام — Grand Total مجموع Total	رجال Men	نساء Women	المواطنين — Nationals مجموع Total	رجال Men	نساء Women	غير مواطنين — Non-Nationals مجموع Total	رجال Men	نساء Women	المعدل الخام (لكل مائة ألف من السكان) — Rate (per 100 thousand population) مجموع Total	رجال Men	نساء Women	النسبة في المئة — percent مجموع Total	رجال Men	نساء Women
1	234	...	...	...	...	...	...	...	...	13.2	...	...	9.2	...	...
2	317	...	...	...	...	...	...	...	...	17.8	...	...	12.4	...	...
3	38	...	...	...	...	...	...	...	...	2.1	...	...	1.5	...	...
4	12	...	...	...	...	...	...	...	...	0.7	...	...	0.5	...	...
5	3	...	...	...	...	...	...	...	...	0.2	...	...	0.1	...	...
6	46	...	...	...	...	...	...	...	...	2.6	...	...	1.8	...	...
7	885	...	...	...	...	...	...	...	...	49.8	...	...	34.7	...	...
8	191	...	...	...	...	...	...	...	...	10.7	...	...	7.5	...	...
9	98	...	...	...	...	...	...	...	...	5.5	...	...	3.8	...	...
10	53	...	...	...	...	...	...	...	...	3.0	...	...	2.1	...	...
11	2	...	...	...	...	...	...	...	...	0.1	...	...	0.1	...	...
12	6	...	...	...	...	...	...	...	...	0.3	...	...	0.2	...	...
13	10	...	...	...	...	...	...	...	...	0.6	...	...	0.4	...	...
14	132	...	...	...	...	...	...	...	...	7.4	...	...	5.2	...	...
15	195	...	...	...	...	...	...	...	...	11.0	...	...	7.7	...	...
16	116	...	...	...	...	...	...	...	...	6.5	...	...	4.6	...	...
17	208	...	...	...	...	...	...	...	...	11.7	...	...	8.2	...	...
18	1	...	...	...	...	...	...	...	...	0.1	...	...	0.0	...	...
المجموع Total	2547	1593	1008	...	...	...	...	...	...	143.3	176.3	115.3	100.0	100.0	100.0
حجم السكان ² Population Size ¹¹	1777685	903328	874357							100000	100000	100000			

¹ Causes of death given in annex 1 — أسباب الوفيات في الملحق رقم 1
¹¹ National population estimates — تقديرات السكان: مصادر وطنية
* Causes of deaths are for the deads in the hospital — الوفيات حسب السبب للمتوفين في المستشفيات

جدول 16 (تابع): أسباب الوفيات المسجلة : المعدل الخام والنسبة في المئة

Table 16 (cont'd): Registered Deaths by Cause: Crude Rates and Per Cent

فلسطين* PALESTINE* — 2005

سبب الوفاة cause of death [I]	المجموع العام Grand Total			المواطنون Nationals			غير مواطنين Non-Nationals			المعدل الخام (لكل مائة ألف من السكان) Rate (per 100 thousand population)			النسبة في المئة percent		
	مجموع Total	رجال Men	نساء Women	مجموع Total	رجال Men	نساء Women	مجموع Total	رجال Men	نساء Women	مجموع Total	رجال Men	نساء Women	مجموع Total	رجال Men	نساء Women
1	378	195	183	...	...	...	...	...	...	10.2	10.4	10.1	3.7	3.5	4.0
2	1042	589	453	...	...	...	...	...	...	28.1	31.3	24.9	10.3	10.6	9.9
3	405	189	216	...	...	...	...	...	...	10.9	10.0	11.9	4.0	3.4	4.7
4	...	...	...	...	...	...	...	...	...	...	...	...	...	...	...
5	...	...	...	...	...	...	...	...	...	...	...	...	...	...	...
6	128	66	62	...	...	...	...	...	...	3.5	3.5	3.4	1.3	1.2	1.4
7	3773	1943	1830	...	...	...	...	...	...	101.9	103.2	100.6	37.2	34.9	40.1
8	696	380	316	...	...	...	...	...	...	18.8	20.2	17.4	6.9	6.8	6.9
9	103	60	43	...	...	...	...	...	...	2.8	3.2	2.4	1.0	1.1	0.9
10	405	208	197	...	...	...	...	...	...	10.9	11.0	10.8	4.0	3.7	4.3
11	1	0	1	...	...	...	...	...	...	0.0	0.0	0.1	0.0	0.0	0.0
12	...	...	...	...	...	...	...	...	...	...	...	...	...	...	...
13	...	...	...	...	...	...	...	...	...	...	...	...	...	...	...
14	504	257	247	...	...	...	...	...	...	13.6	13.6	13.6	5.0	4.6	5.4
15	874	490	384	...	...	...	...	...	...	23.6	26.0	21.1	8.6	8.8	8.4
16	573	283	290	...	...	...	...	...	...	15.5	15.0	15.9	5.7	5.1	6.3
17	...	...	...	...	...	...	...	...	...	...	...	...	...	...	...
18	...	...	...	...	...	...	...	...	...	...	...	...	...	...	...
19	...	...	...	...	...	...	...	...	...	...	...	...	...	...	...
20	...	...	...	...	...	...	...	...	...	...	...	...	...	...	...
21	547	447	100	...	...	...	...	...	...	14.8	23.7	5.5	5.4	8.0	2.2
22	707	462	245	...	...	...	...	...	...	19.1	24.5	13.5	7.0	8.3	5.4
المجموع Total	10136	5569	4567	...	...	...	...	...	...	273.8	295.8	251.1	100.0	100.0	100.0
حجم السكان Population Size [II]	3702000	1883000	1819000							100000	100000	100000			

I Causes of death given in annex 1

II World Population Prospects - 2004 Revision.

* The source for the causes of deaths in this table is Population register (discrepency with the number in the table 4)

[I] أسباب الوفيات في ملحق رقم 1

[II] أفاق سكان العالم – مراجعة عام 2004.

* مصدر أسباب الوفيات في هذا الجدول من تسجيل السكان (ويختلف مع الرقم المذكور في الجدول 4)

جدول 16 (تابع): أسباب الوفيات المسجلة : المعدل الخام والنسبة في المئة
Table 16 (cont'd): Registered Deaths by Cause: Crude Rates and Per Cent

فلسطين* PALESTINE*
2004

سبب الوفاة [1] cause of death [1]	المجموع العام Grand Total			المواطنون Nationals			غير مواطنين Non-Nationals			المعدل الخام (لكل مائة ألف من السكان) Rate (per 100 thousand population)			النسبة في المئة percent		
	محموع Total	رجال Men	نساء Women	محموع Total	رجال Men	نساء Women	محموع Total	رجال Men	نساء Women	محموع Total	رجال Men	نساء Women	محموع Total	رجال Men	نساء Women
1	382	217	165	…	…	…	…	…	…	10.6	11.9	9.4	3.7	3.6	3.8
2	1036	579	457	…	…	…	…	…	…	28.9	31.7	25.9	10.0	9.7	10.5
3	454	210	244	…	…	…	…	…	…	12.7	11.5	13.8	4.4	3.5	5.6
4	…	…	…	…	…	…	…	…	…	…	…	…	…	…	…
5	…	…	…	…	…	…	…	…	…	…	…	…	…	…	…
6	133	69	64	…	…	…	…	…	…	3.7	3.8	3.6	1.3	1.2	1.5
7	3471	1773	1698	…	…	…	…	…	…	96.8	97.2	96.3	33.6	29.7	39.0
8	664	404	260	…	…	…	…	…	…	18.5	22.1	14.7	6.4	6.8	6.0
9	108	64	44	…	…	…	…	…	…	3.0	3.5	2.5	1.0	1.1	1.0
10	351	198	153	…	…	…	…	…	…	9.8	10.9	8.7	3.4	3.3	3.5
11	3	0	3	…	…	…	…	…	…	0.1	0.0	0.2	0.0	0.0	0.1
12	…	…	…	…	…	…	…	…	…	…	…	…	…	…	…
13	…	…	…	…	…	…	…	…	…	…	…	…	…	…	…
14	468	237	231	…	…	…	…	…	…	13.0	13.0	13.1	4.5	4.0	5.3
15	825	469	356	…	…	…	…	…	…	23.0	25.7	20.2	8.0	7.9	8.2
16	603	307	296	…	…	…	…	…	…	16.8	16.8	16.8	5.8	5.1	6.8
17	…	…	…	…	…	…	…	…	…	…	…	…	…	…	…
18	…	…	…	…	…	…	…	…	…	…	…	…	…	…	…
19	…	…	…	…	…	…	…	…	…	…	…	…	…	…	…
20	…	…	…	…	…	…	…	…	…	…	…	…	…	…	…
21	1173	1048	125	…	…	…	…	…	…	32.7	57.5	7.1	11.4	17.5	2.9
22	655	397	258	…	…	…	…	…	…	18.3	21.8	14.6	6.3	6.6	5.9
المجموع Total	10326	5972	4354	…	…	…	…	…	…	287.9	327.4	247.0	100.0	100.0	100.0
حجم السكان [II] Population Size [II]	3587000	1824000	1763000	…						100000	100000	100000	100000	100000	

[1] Causes of death given in annex 1
[II] World Population Prospects - 2004 Revision.
* The source for the causes of deaths in this table is Population register (discrepency with the number in the table 4)

1 أسباب الوفيات في الملحق رقم 1
II آفاق سكان العالم - مراجعة عام 2004.
* مصدر أسباب الوفيات في هذا الجدول من تسجيل السكان (ويختلف مع الرقم المذكور في الجدول 4)

جدول 16 (تابع): أسباب الوفيات المسجلة : المعدل الخام والنسبة في المئة

Table 16 (cont'd): Registered Deaths by Cause: Crude Rates and Per Cent

PALESTINE* فلسطين* 2003 سبب الوفاة cause of death[1]	المجموع العام Grand Total			المواطنون Nationals			غير مواطنين Non-Nationals			المعدل الخام (لكل مائة ألف من السكان) Rate (per 100 thousand population)			النسبة في المئة percent		
	مجموع Total	رجال Men	نساء Women	مجموع Total	رجال Men	نساء Women	مجموع Total	رجال Men	نساء Women	مجموع Total	رجال Men	نساء Women	مجموع Total	رجال Men	نساء Women
1	300	172	128	...	...	...	...	...	...	8.4	9.5	7.3	2.9	3.0	2.8
2	918	481	437	...	...	...	...	...	...	25.8	26.6	25.0	9.0	8.5	9.7
3	492	194	298	...	...	...	...	...	...	13.8	10.7	17.0	4.8	3.4	6.6
4	...	...	...	...	...	...	...	...	...	...	...	...	...	...	...
5				...	...	...	...	...	...						
6	138	75	63	...	...	...	...	...	...	3.9	4.1	3.6	1.4	1.3	1.4
7	3717	1951	1766	...	...	...	...	...	...	104.5	107.8	101.0	36.5	34.4	39.2
8	490	289	201	...	...	...	...	...	...	13.8	16.0	11.5	4.8	5.1	4.5
9	102	67	35	...	...	...	...	...	...	2.9	3.7	2.0	1.0	1.2	0.8
10	343	182	161	...	...	...	...	...	...	9.6	10.1	9.2	3.4	3.2	3.6
11	7	0	7	...	...	...	...	...	...	0.2	0.0	0.4	0.1	0.0	0.2
12	...	...	...	...	...	...	...	...	...	...	...	...	...	...	...
13	...	...	...	...	...	...	...	...	...	...	...	...	...	...	...
14	328	171	157	...	...	...	...	...	...	9.2	9.5	9.0	3.2	3.0	3.5
15	989	539	450	...	...	...	...	...	...	27.8	29.8	25.7	9.7	9.5	10.0
16	697	346	351	...	...	...	...	...	...	19.6	19.1	20.1	6.8	6.1	7.8
17	...	...	...	...	...	...	...	...	...	...	...	...	...	...	...
18	...	...	...	...	...	...	...	...	...	...	...	...	...	...	...
19	...	...	...	...	...	...	...	...	...	...	...	...	...	...	...
20	...	...	...	...	...	...	...	...	...	...	...	...	...	...	...
21	904	803	101	...	...	...	...	...	...	25.4	44.4	5.8	8.9	14.2	2.2
22	759	404	355	...	...	...	...	...	...	21.3	22.3	20.3	7.5	7.1	7.9
المجموع Total	10184	5674	4510	...			...			286.3	313.7	258.0	100.0	100.0	100.0
حجم السكان Population Size[II]	3557000	1809000	1748000	1748000			100000	100000		100000	100000	100000			

[I] Causes of death given in annex 1 — أسباب الوفيات في الملحق رقم 1
[II] World Population Prospects - 2002 Revision. — اتفاق سكان العالم – مراجعة عام 2002.
* The source for the causes of deaths in this table is Population register (discrepency with the number in the table 4) — مصدر أسباب الوفيات في هذا الجدول من تسجيل السكان (بتطابق مع الرقم المذكور في الجدول 4)

-62-

جدول 16 (تابع): أسباب الوفيات المسجلة : المعدل الخام والنسبة في المئة

Table 16 (cont'd): Registered Deaths by Cause: Crude Rates and Per Cent

PALESTINE / فلسطين

2002

سبب الوفاة / cause of death [I]	المجموع العام / Grand Total			المواطنون / Nationals			غير مواطنين / Non-Nationals			المعدل الخام (لكل مائة ألف من السكان) / Rate (per 100 thousand population)			النسبة في المئة / percent		
	مجموع ع / Total	رجال / Men	نساء / Women	مجموع ع / Total	رجال / Men	نساء / Women	مجموع ع / Total	رجال / Men	نساء / Women	مجموع ع / Total	رجال / Men	نساء / Women	مجموع ع / Total	رجال / Men	نساء / Women
1	407	278	129	...	...	...	...	...	...	11.9	15.9	7.6	3.8	4.4	2.9
2	886	488	398	...	...	...	...	...	...	25.8	27.9	23.6	8.2	7.7	9.0
3	596	290	306	...	...	...	...	...	...	17.4	16.6	18.1	5.5	4.6	6.9
4	...	...	...	...	...	...	...	...	...	...	...	...	...	...	...
5	...	...	...	...	...	...	...	...	...	...	...	...	...	...	...
6	119	63	56	...	...	...	...	...	...	3.5	3.6	3.3	1.1	1.0	1.3
7*	3762	1973	1789	...	...	...	...	...	...	109.6	113.0	106.0	34.8	31.0	40.3
8	378	234	144	...	...	...	...	...	...	11.0	13.4	8.5	3.5	3.7	3.2
9	...	...	...	...	...	...	...	...	...	...	...	...	...	...	...
10**	267	138	129	...	...	...	...	...	...	7.8	7.9	7.6	2.5	2.2	2.9
11	4	0	4	...	...	...	...	...	...	0.1	0.0	0.2	0.0	0.0	0.1
12	...	...	...	...	...	...	...	...	...	...	...	...	...	...	...
13	...	...	...	...	...	...	...	...	...	...	...	...	...	...	...
14	389	206	183	...	...	...	...	...	...	11.3	11.8	10.8	3.6	3.2	4.1
15	1264	705	559	...	...	...	...	...	...	36.8	40.4	33.1	11.7	11.1	12.6
16	...	...	...	...	...	...	...	...	...	...	...	...	...	...	...
17	1349	1190	159	...	...	...	...	...	...	39.3	68.2	9.4	12.5	18.7	3.6
18***	1384	801	583	...	...	...	...	...	...	40.3	45.9	34.6	12.8	12.6	13.1
المجموع / Total	10805	6366	4439	...	...	...	...	...	...	314.7	364.6	263.1	100.0	100.0	100.0
حجم السكان / Population Size [II]	3433000	1746000	1687000							100000	100000	100000			

I Causes of death given in annex I / أسباب الوفيات في الملحق رقم 1

* includes heart disease and hypertension / تشمل امراض القلب وضغط الدم

** includes kidney failure only / تشمل الفشل الكلوي فقط

*** others / اخرى

II World Population Prospects - 2002 Revision. / آفاق سكان العالم – مراجعة عام 2002.

-63-

جدول 16 (تابع): أسباب الوفيات المسجلة : المعدل الخام والنسبة في المئة

Table 16 (cont'd): Registered Deaths by Cause: Crude Rates and Per Cent

PALESTINE 2001 / cause of death [I]	Grand Total			Nationals			Non-Nationals			Rate (per 100 thousand population)			percent		
	Total	Men	Women	Total	Men	Women	Total	Men	Women	Total	Men	Women	Total	Men	Women
1	176	84	92	...	...	...	...	...	...	5.3	5.0	5.7	1.9	1.7	2.2
2	969	507	462	...	...	...	...	...	...	29.3	30.1	28.4	10.5	10.1	11.0
3	579	257	322	...	...	...	...	...	...	17.5	15.3	19.8	6.3	5.1	7.7
4	...	...	...	...	...	...	...	...	...	...	...	...	...	...	...
5	...	...	...	...	...	...	...	...	...	...	...	...	...	...	...
6	117	58	59	...	...	...	...	...	...	3.5	3.4	3.6	1.3	1.2	1.4
7*	3509	1748	1761	...	...	...	...	...	...	106.0	103.9	108.2	38.0	34.7	42.1
8	432	246	186	...	...	...	...	...	...	13.0	14.6	11.4	4.7	4.9	4.4
9	...	...	...	...	...	...	...	...	...	...	...	...	...	...	...
10**	227	125	102	...	...	...	...	...	...	6.9	7.4	6.3	2.5	2.5	2.4
11	5	0	5	...	...	...	...	...	...	0.2	0.0	0.3	0.1	0.0	0.1
12	...	...	...	...	...	...	...	...	...	...	...	...	...	...	...
13	...	...	...	...	...	...	...	...	...	...	...	...	...	...	...
14	402	209	193	...	...	...	...	...	...	12.1	12.4	11.9	4.4	4.1	4.6
15	590	335	255	...	...	...	...	...	...	17.8	19.9	15.7	6.4	6.6	6.1
16	...	...	...	...	...	...	...	...	...	...	...	...	...	...	...
17	718	630	88	...	...	...	...	...	...	21.7	37.4	5.4	7.8	12.5	2.1
18***	1499	839	660	...	...	...	...	...	...	45.3	49.9	40.5	16.3	16.7	15.8
Total	9223	5038	4185	...	...	...	...	...	...	278.6	299.3	257.1	100.0	100.0	100.0
Population Size [II]	3311000	1683000	1628000							100000	100000	100000			

[I] Causes of death given in annex I

* includes heart disease and hypertension

** includes kidney failure only

*** others

[II] World Population Prospects - 2000 Revision.

أسباب الوفيات في الملحق رقم I

* تشمل امراض القلب وضغط الدم

** تشمل الفشل الكلوي فقط

*** اخرى

آفاق سكان العالم – مراجعة عام 2000.

جدول 16 (تابع): أسباب الوفيات المسجلة : المعدل الخام و النسبة في المئة

Table 16 (cont'd): Registered Deaths by Cause: Crude Rates and Per Cent

cause of death [1] سبب الوفاة [1]	المجموع العام Grand Total			المواطنون Nationals			غير مواطنين Non-Nationals			المعدل الخام (لكل مائة ألف من السكان) Rate (per 100 thousand population)			النسبة في المئة percent		
PALESTINE 2000	مجموع Total	رجال Men	نساء Women	مجموع Total	رجال Men	نساء Women	مجموع Total	رجال Men	نساء Women	مجموع Total	رجال Men	نساء Women	مجموع Total	رجال Men	نساء Women
1	219	125	94	...	...	...	...	...	...	6.9	7.7	6.0	2.4	2.5	2.2
2	848	467	381	...	...	...	...	...	...	26.6	28.8	24.3	9.3	9.5	9.1
3	396	191	205	...	...	...	...	...	...	12.4	11.8	13.1	4.3	3.9	4.9
4	...	...	...	...	...	...	...	...	...	...	...	...	...	...	...
5	...	...	...	...	...	...	...	...	...	...	...	...	...	...	...
6	105	59	46	...	...	...	...	...	...	3.3	3.6	2.9	1.2	1.2	1.1
7*	3508	1806	1702	...	...	...	...	...	...	109.9	111.3	108.5	38.5	36.7	40.5
8	409	224	185	...	...	...	...	...	...	12.8	13.8	11.8	4.5	4.6	4.4
9	...	...	...	...	...	...	...	...	...	...	...	...	...	...	...
10**	277	127	150	...	...	...	...	...	...	8.7	7.8	9.6	3.0	2.6	3.6
11	5	0	5	...	...	...	...	...	...	0.2	0.0	0.3	0.1	0.0	0.1
12	...	...	...	...	...	...	...	...	...	...	...	...	...	...	...
13	...	...	...	...	...	...	...	...	...	...	...	...	...	...	...
14	281	148	133	...	...	...	...	...	...	8.8	9.1	8.5	3.1	3.0	3.2
15	513	287	226	...	...	...	...	...	...	16.1	17.7	14.4	5.6	5.8	5.4
16	...	...	...	...	...	...	...	...	...	...	...	...	...	...	...
17	471	379	92	...	...	...	...	...	...	14.8	23.4	5.9	5.2	7.7	2.2
18***	2086	1104	982	...	...	...	...	...	...	65.4	68.1	62.6	22.9	22.5	23.4
المجموع Total	9118	4917	4201	...	...	...	...	...	...	285.7	303.1	267.8	100.0	100.0	100.0
حجم السكان [II] Population Size [II]	3191000	1622000	1569000	100000	100000					100000	100000	100000			

[1] Causes of death given in annex 1 — أسباب الوفيات في الملحق رقم 1

* includes heart disease and hypertension — تشمل امراض القلب وضغط الدم

** includes kidney failure only — تشمل الفشل الكلوي فقط

*** others — اخرى

[II] World Population Prospects - 2000 Revision. — آفاق سكان العالم – مراجعة عام 2000.

[II] Revised projections based on 1997-Census: (national sources for population estimates) — اسقاطات منقحة حسب تعداد (تقدير ات السكان: مصادر وطنية) 1997

جدول 16 (تابع): أسباب الوفيات المسجلة : المعدل الخام والنسبة في المئة

Table 16 (cont'd): Registered Deaths by Cause: Crude Rates and Per Cent

قطر QATAR 2006

سبب الوفاة cause of death [1]	المجموع العام Grand Total			المواطنون Nationals			غير مواطنين Non-Nationals			المعدل الخام (لكل مائة ألف من السكان) Rate (per 100 thousand population)			النسبة في المئة percent		
	مجموع Total	رجال Men	نساء Women	مجموع Total	رجال Men	نساء Women	مجموع Total	رجال Men	نساء Women	مجموع Total	رجال Men	نساء Women	مجموع Total	رجال Men	نساء Women
1	12	7	5	6	3	3	6	4	2	1.5	1.3	1.9	0.7	0.5	1.1
2	157	87	70	62	25	37	95	62	33	19.1	15.8	25.9	9.0	6.8	14.7
3	114	62	52	72	35	37	42	27	15	13.9	11.2	19.3	6.5	4.9	10.9
4	7	4	3	4	1	3	3	3	0	0.9	0.7	1.1	0.4	0.3	0.6
5	1	1	0	1	1	0	0	0	0	0.1	0.2	0.0	0.1	0.1	0.0
6	28	15	13	9	4	5	19	11	8	3.4	2.7	4.8	1.6	1.2	2.7
7	324	186	138	171	82	89	153	104	49	39.4	33.7	51.1	18.5	14.6	29.0
8	63	34	29	35	18	17	28	16	12	7.7	6.2	10.7	3.6	2.7	6.1
9	48	35	13	19	12	7	29	23	6	5.8	6.3	4.8	2.7	2.7	2.7
10	31	18	13	20	11	9	11	7	4	3.8	3.3	4.8	1.8	1.4	2.7
11	1	0	1	0	0	0	1	0	1	0.1	0.0	0.4	0.1	0.0	0.2
12	4	2	2	3	2	1	1	0	1	0.5	0.4	0.7	0.2	0.2	0.4
13	2	1	1	0	0	0	2	1	1	0.2	0.2	0.4	0.1	0.1	0.2
14	48	23	25	22	12	10	26	11	15	5.8	4.2	9.3	2.7	1.8	5.3
15	54	30	24	28	18	10	26	12	14	6.6	5.4	8.9	3.1	2.4	5.0
16	384	342	42	87	63	24	297	279	18	46.7	62.0	15.6	21.9	26.8	8.8
17	0	0	0	0	0	0	0	0	0	0.0	0.0	0.0	0.0	0.0	0.0
18	472	427	45	137	112	25	335	315	20	57.4	77.4	16.7	27.0	33.5	9.5
المجموع Total	1750	1274	476	676	399	277	1074	875	199	212.9	230.8	176.3	100.0	100.0	100.0
حجم السكان Population Size [II]	822000	552000	270000							100000	100000	100000			

[1] أسباب الوفيات في الملحق رقم 1
[1] Causes of death given in annex 1

[II] أفاق سكان العالم - مراجعة عام 2006.
[II] World Population Prospects - The 2006 Revision.

جدول 16 (تابع): أسباب الوفيات المسجلة : المعدل الخام والنسبة في المئة

Table 16 (cont'd): Registered Deaths by Cause: Crude Rates and Per Cent

QATAR 2005 / cause of death [I]	Grand Total Total	Men	Women	Nationals Total	Men	Women	Non-Nationals Total	Men	Women	Rate (per 100 thousand population) Total	Men	Women	percent Total	Men	Women
1	12	7	5	1	0	1	11	7	4	1.5	1.3	1.9	0.8	0.6	1.1
2	162	102	60	81	51	30	81	51	30	20.0	18.6	22.6	10.5	9.2	13.7
3	109	56	53	69	35	34	40	21	19	13.4	10.2	20.0	7.1	5.1	12.1
4	11	7	4	7	3	4	4	4	0	1.4	1.3	1.5	0.7	0.6	0.9
5	0	0	0	0	0	0	0	0	0	0.0	0.0	0.0	0.0	0.0	0.0
6	15	9	6	8	5	3	7	4	3	1.8	1.6	2.3	1.0	0.8	1.4
7	314	203	111	184	108	76	130	95	35	38.7	37.1	41.9	20.3	18.3	25.4
8	61	32	29	36	16	20	25	16	9	7.5	5.9	10.9	3.9	2.9	6.6
9	36	29	7	16	11	5	20	18	2	4.4	5.3	2.6	2.3	2.6	1.6
10	44	26	18	21	10	11	23	16	7	5.4	4.8	6.8	2.8	2.3	4.1
11	3	0	3	1	0	1	2	0	2	0.4	0.0	1.1	0.2	0.0	0.7
12	13	8	5	9	5	4	4	3	1	1.6	1.5	1.9	0.8	0.7	1.1
13	0	0	0	0	0	0	0	0	0	0.0	0.0	0.0	0.0	0.0	0.0
14	39	19	20	20	9	11	19	10	9	4.8	3.5	7.5	2.5	1.7	4.6
15	48	27	21	22	13	9	26	14	12	5.9	4.9	7.9	3.1	2.4	4.8
16	340	286	54	96	64	32	244	222	22	41.9	52.3	20.4	22.0	25.8	12.4
17	0	0	0	0	0	0	0	0	0	0.0	0.0	0.0	0.0	0.0	0.0
18	338	297	41	111	90	21	227	207	20	41.6	54.3	15.5	21.9	26.8	9.4
Total	1545	1108	437	682	420	262	863	688	175	190.3	202.6	164.9	100.0	100.0	100.0
Population Size [II]	812000	547000	265000			265000				100000	100000	100000			

[I] Causes of death given in annex 1
[II] "World Population Prospects – The 2004 Revision.

أسباب الوفيات في الملحق رقم 1
آفاق سكان العالم – مراجعة عام 2004.

-67-

جدول 16 (تابع): أسباب الوفيات المسجلة : المعدل الخام والنسبة في المئة

Table 16 (cont'd): Registered Deaths by Cause: Crude Rates and Per Cent

قطر QATAR 2004 سبب الوفاة cause of death [1]	المجموع العام Grand Total			المواطنون Nationals			غير مواطنين Non-Nationals			المعدل الخام (لكل مائة ألف من السكان) Rate (per 100 thousand population)			النسبة في المئة percent		
	مجموع Total	رجال Men	نساء Women	مجموع Total	رجال Men	نساء Women	مجموع Total	رجال Men	نساء Women	مجموع Total	رجال Men	نساء Women	مجموع Total	رجال Men	نساء Women
1	25	14	11	15	7	8	10	7	3	3.2	2.7	4.3	1.9	.5	2.6
2	137	77	60	80	42	38	57	35	22	17.6	14.8	23.4	10.2	8.3	14.4
3	92	49	43	68	31	37	24	18	6	11.8	9.4	16.8	6.9	5.3	10.3
4	4	2	2	2	1	1	2	1	1	0.5	0.4	0.8	0.3	.2	0.5
5	1	0	1	1	0	1	0	0	0	0.1	0.0	0.4	0.1	.0	0.2
6	22	13	9	12	6	6	10	7	3	2.8	2.5	3.5	1.6	.4	2.2
7	256	154	102	159	86	73	97	68	29	32.9	29.6	39.8	19.1	16.7	24.5
8	86	52	34	57	35	22	29	17	12	11.1	10.0	13.3	6.4	5.6	8.2
9	24	18	6	13	10	3	11	8	3	3.1	3.5	2.3	1.8	1.9	1.4
10	47	21	26	37	15	22	10	6	4	6.0	4.0	10.2	3.5	2.3	6.2
11	1	0	1	0	0	0	1	0	1	0.1	0.0	0.4	0.1	.0	0.2
12	6	4	2	5	3	2	1	1	0	0.8	0.8	0.8	0.4	.4	0.5
13	0	0	0	0	0	0	0	0	0	0.0	0.0	0.0	0.0	.0	0.0
14	44	22	22	21	13	8	23	9	14	5.7	4.2	8.6	3.3	2.4	5.3
15	54	30	24	22	14	8	32	16	16	6.9	5.8	9.4	4.0	3.2	5.8
16	263	218	45	76	49	27	187	169	18	33.8	41.8	17.6	19.6	23.6	10.8
17	0	0	0	0	0	0	0	0	0	0.0	0.0	0.0	0.0	.0	0.0
18	279	250	29	89	73	16	190	177	13	35.9	48.0	11.3	20.8	27.1	7.0
المجموع Total	1341	924	417	657	385	272	684	539	145	172.6	177.4	162.9	100.0	100.0	100.0
حجم السكان Population Size [II]	777000	521000	256000				100000	100000	100000	100000	100000	100000			

-68-

[1] Causes of death given in annex 1 — أسباب الوفيات في ملحق رقم 1
[II] "World Population Prospects - The 2004 Revision." — "آفاق سكان العالم - حجمة عام 2004."

جدول 16 (تابع) : أسباب الوفيات المسجلة : المعدل الخام والنسبة في المئة

Table 16 (cont'd): Registered Deaths by Cause: Crude Rates and Per Cent

قطر QATAR
2003

سبب الوفاة[I] cause of death	المجموع العام Grand Total			المواطنون Nationals			غير مواطنين Non-Nationals			المعدل الخام (لكل مائة ألف من السكان) Rate (per 100 thousand population)			النسبة في المئة percent		
	مجموع Total	رجال Men	نساء Women	مجموع Total	رجال Men	نساء Women	مجموع Total	رجال Men	نساء Women	مجموع Total	رجال Men	نساء Women	مجموع Total	رجال Men	نساء Women
1	36	22	14	16	8	8	20	14	6	5.9	5.7	6.3	2.7	2.5	3.4
2	116	67	49	60	34	26	56	33	23	19.0	17.3	22.0	8.8	7.5	11.8
3	156	95	61	101	59	42	55	36	19	25.6	24.5	27.4	11.9	10.6	14.7
4	9	6	3	3	1	2	6	5	1	1.5	1.6	1.3	0.7	0.7	0.7
5	4	2	2	3	2	1	1	0	1	0.7	0.5	0.9	0.3	0.2	0.5
6	20	13	7	13	7	6	7	6	1	3.3	3.4	3.1	1.5	1.5	1.7
7	276	172	104	137	74	63	139	98	41	45.2	44.4	46.6	21.1	19.2	25.1
8	41	27	14	23	13	10	18	14	4	6.7	7.0	6.3	3.1	3.0	3.4
9	21	11	10	8	5	3	13	6	7	3.4	2.8	4.5	1.6	1.2	2.4
10	20	9	11	13	5	8	7	4	3	3.3	2.3	4.9	1.5	1.0	2.7
11	3	0	3	2	0	2	1	0	1	0.5	0.0	1.3	0.2	0.0	0.7
12	9	3	6	5	3	2	4	0	4	1.5	0.8	2.7	0.7	0.3	1.4
13	1	1	0	1	1	0	0	0	0	0.2	0.3	0.0	0.1	0.1	0.0
14	75	37	38	43	21	22	32	16	16	12.3	9.6	17.0	5.7	4.1	9.2
15	55	33	22	35	19	16	20	14	6	9.0	8.5	9.9	4.2	3.7	5.3
16	235	192	43	67	41	26	168	151	17	38.5	49.6	19.3	17.9	21.4	10.4
17	22	17	5	6	5	1	16	12	4	3.6	4.4	2.2	1.7	1.9	1.2
18	212	189	23	82	72	10	130	117	13	34.8	48.8	10.3	16.2	21.1	5.5
المجموع Total	1311	896	415	618	370	248	693	526	167	214.9	231.5	186.1	100.0	100.0	100.0
حجم السكان[II] Population Size	610000	387000	223000	100000			100000	100000							

[I] Causes of death given in annex 1
[II] "World Population Prospects - The 2002 Revision."

[I] أسباب الوفيات في الملحق رقم 1
[II] "آفاق سكان العالم - مراجعة عام 2002."

قطر QATAR

2002

سبب الوفاة cause of death [1]	المجموع العام Grand Total			المواطنون Nationals			غير مواطنين Non-Nationals			المعدل الخام (لكل مائة ألف من السكان) Rate (per 100 thousand population)			النسبة في المئة percent		
	مجموع Total	رجال Men	نساء Women	مجموع Total	رجال Men	نساء Women	مجموع Total	رجال Men	نساء Women	مجموع Total	رجال Men	نساء Women	مجموع Total	رجال Men	نساء Women
1	43	29	14	26	16	10	17	13	4	7.2	7.6	6.4	3.5	3.4	3.8
2	128	69	59	79	40	39	49	29	20	21.3	18.0	27.1	10.5	8.1	16.2
3	92	61	31	68	43	25	24	18	6	15.3	15.9	14.2	7.5	7.1	8.5
4	8	2	6	5	1	4	3	1	2	1.3	0.5	2.8	0.7	0.2	1.6
5	3	1	2	3	1	2	0	0	0	0.5	0.3	0.9	0.2	0.1	0.5
6	26	18	8	15	11	4	11	7	4	4.3	4.7	3.7	2.1	2.1	2.2
7	271	178	93	151	82	69	120	96	24	45.1	46.5	42.7	22.2	20.8	25.5
8	59	36	23	47	29	18	12	7	5	9.8	9.4	10.6	4.8	4.2	6.3
9	24	16	8	10	5	5	14	11	3	4.0	4.2	3.7	2.0	.9	2.2
10	51	31	20	35	20	15	16	11	5	8.5	8.1	9.2	4.2	3.6	5.5
11	0	0	0	0	0	0	0	0	0	0.0	0.0	0.0	0.0	0.0	0.0
12	1	0	1	1	0	1	0	0	0	0.2	0.0	0.5	0.1	0.0	0.3
13	2	1	1	1	0	1	1	1	0	0.3	0.3	0.5	0.2	0.1	0.3
14	58	32	26	33	17	16	25	15	10	9.7	8.4	11.9	4.8	3.7	7.1
15	35	23	12	24	16	8	11	7	4	5.8	6.0	5.5	2.9	2.7	3.3
16	208	178	30	74	52	22	134	126	8	34.6	46.5	13.8	17.0	20.8	8.2
17	21	15	6	7	4	3	14	11	3	3.5	3.9	2.8	1.7	1.8	1.6
18	190	165	25	85	69	16	105	96	9	31.6	43.1	11.5	15.6	19.3	6.8
المجموع Total	1220	855	365	664	406	258	556	449	107	203.0	223.2	167.4	100.0	100.0	100.0
حجم السكان Population Size [2]	601000	383000	218000	100000			100000			100000					

[1] Causes of death given in annex 1 أسباب الوفيات في الملحق رقم 1

[2] World Population Prospects - The 2000 Revision. آفاق سكان العالم - مراجعة عام 2000.

-70-

جدول 16 (تابع): أسباب الوفيات المسجلة : المعدل الخام والنسبة في المئة

Table 16 (cont'd): Registered Deaths by Cause: Crude Rates and Per Cent

قطر QATAR 2001 سبب الوفاة [I] cause of death [I]	المجموع العام Grand Total			المواطنون Nationals			غير مواطنين Non-Nationals			المعدل الخام (لكل مائة ألف من السكان) Rate (per 100 thousand population)			النسبة في الألف percent		
	مجموع Total	رجال Men	نساء Women	مجموع Total	رجال Men	نساء Women	مجموع Total	رجال Men	نساء Women	مجموع Total	رجال Men	نساء Women	مجموع Total	رجال Men	نساء Women
1	53	36	17	25	22	3	28	14	14	9.2	9.7	8.3	4.4	4.3	4.5
2	95	58	37	30	20	10	65	38	27	16.5	15.6	18.1	7.9	7.0	9.8
3	88	52	36	34	25	9	54	27	27	15.3	14.0	17.6	7.3	6.3	9.5
4	4	2	2	0	0	0	4	2	2	0.7	0.5	1.0	0.3	0.2	0.5
5	9	4	5	2	1	1	7	3	4	1.6	1.1	2.5	0.7	0.5	1.3
6	23	12	11	9	5	4	14	7	7	4.0	3.2	5.4	1.9	1.4	2.9
7	456	343	113	236	205	31	220	138	82	79.3	92.5	55.4	37.7	41.3	29.8
8	51	27	24	19	13	6	32	14	18	8.9	7.3	11.8	4.2	3.2	6.3
9	27	17	10	14	12	2	13	5	8	4.7	4.6	4.9	2.2	2.0	2.6
10	51	28	23	24	17	7	27	11	16	8.9	7.5	11.3	4.2	3.4	6.1
11	1	0	1	0	0	0	1	0	1	0.2	0.0	0.5	0.1	0.0	0.3
12	1	1	0	0	0	0	1	1	0	0.2	0.3	0.0	0.1	0.1	0.0
13	5	2	3	4	2	2	1	0	1	0.9	0.5	1.5	0.4	0.2	0.8
14	46	27	19	23	11	12	23	16	7	8.0	7.3	9.3	3.8	3.2	5.0
15	41	18	23	23	10	13	18	8	10	7.1	4.9	11.3	3.4	2.2	6.1
16	47	25	22	15	11	4	32	14	18	8.2	6.7	10.8	3.9	3.0	5.8
17	207	175	32	132	112	20	75	63	12	36.0	47.2	15.7	17.1	21.1	8.4
18	5	4	1	2	2	0	3	2	1	0.9	1.1	0.5	0.4	0.5	0.3
المجموع Total	1210	831	379	592	468	124	618	363	255	210.4	224.0	185.8	100.0	100.0	100.0
حجم السكان [II] Population Size [II]	575000	371000	204000	204000						100000	100000	100000			

[I] أسباب الوفيات في الملحق رقم 1

[II] "آفاق سكان العالم – مراجعة عام 2000."

[I] Causes of death given in annex 1

[II] "World Population Prospects - The 2000 Revision."

جدول 16 (تابع): المعدل الخام والنسبة في المئة

Table 16 (cont'd): Registered Deaths by Cause: Crude Rates and Per Cent

قطر / QATAR — 2000

أسباب الوفيات المسجلة : المعدل الخام والنسبة في المئة

cause of death I سبب الوفاة	المجموع العام Grand Total			المواطنون Nationals			غير مواطنين Non-Nationals			المعدل الخام Rate (per 100 thousand population)			النسبة في المئة Ratio (per %)		
	مجموع Total	رجال Men	نساء Women	مجموع Total	رجال Men	نساء Women	مجموع Total	رجال Men	نساء Women	مجموع Total	رجال Men	نساء Women	مجموع Total	رجال Mer	نساء Women
1	47	35	12	30	20	10	17	15	2	8.3	9.6	6.0	4.0	4.5	3.0
2	129	63	66	85	40	45	44	23	21	22.8	17.2	33.2	11.0	8.1	16.8
3	75	43	32	56	32	24	19	11	8	13.3	11.7	16.1	6.4	5.5	8.1
4	8	4	4	3	1	2	5	3	2	1.4	1.1	2.0	0.7	0.5	1.0
5	5	2	3	4	1	3	1	1	0	0.9	0.5	1.5	0.4	0.3	0.8
6	20	7	13	8	2	6	12	5	7	3.5	1.9	6.5	1.7	0.9	3.3
7	350	250	100	175	103	72	175	147	28	61.9	68.3	50.3	29.8	32.1	25.4
8	51	31	20	36	20	16	15	11	4	9.0	8.5	10.1	4.3	4.0	5.1
9	30	17	13	14	5	9	16	12	4	5.3	4.6	6.5	2.6	2.2	3.3
10	65	40	25	43	23	20	22	17	5	11.5	10.9	12.6	5.5	5.1	6.3
11	0	0	0	0	0	0	0	0	0	0.0	0.0	0.0	0.0	0.0	0.0
12	0	0	0	0	0	0	0	0	0	0.0	0.0	0.0	0.0	0.0	0.0
13	5	1	4	1	0	1	4	1	3	0.9	0.3	2.0	0.4	0.1	1.0
14	57	22	35	29	10	19	28	12	16	10.1	6.0	17.6	4.9	2.8	8.9
15	52	34	18	25	17	8	27	17	10	9.2	9.3	9.0	4.4	4.4	4.6
16	103	76	27	34	20	14	69	56	13	18.2	20.8	13.6	8.8	9.8	6.9
17	176	154	22	71	58	13	105	96	9	31.2	42.1	11.1	15.0	19.8	5.6
18	0	0	0	0	0	0	0	0	0	0.0	0.0	0.0	0.0	0.0	0.0
المجموع Total	1173	779	394	614	352	262	559	427	132	207.6	212.8	198.0	100.0	100.0	100.0
حجم السكان Population Size II	565000	366000	199000							100000	100000	100000			

I Causes of death given in annex 1 — أسباب الوفيات في الملحق رقم 1

II "World Population Prospects - The 2000 Revision." — آفاق سكان العالم – مراجعة عام 2000.

جدول 16 (تابع): أسباب الوفيات المسجلة : المعدل الخام والنسبة في المئة

Table 16 (cont'd): Registered Deaths by Cause: Crude Rates and Per Cent

الإمارات العربية المتحدة
UNITED ARAB EMIRATES
2000

سبب الوفاة cause of death	المجموع العام Grand Total			المواطنون Nationals			غير مواطنين Non-Nationals			المعدل الخام Rate (per 100 thousand population)			النسبة في المئة Ratio (per %)		
	مجموع Total	رجال Men	نساء Women	مجموع Total	رجال Men	نساء Women	مجموع Total	رجال Men	نساء Women	مجموع Total	رجال Men	نساء Women	مجموع Total	رجال Men	نساء Women
1	41	25	16	15	10	5	26	15	11	1.6	1.5	1.8	0.8	0.6	1.1
2	468	268	200	194	106	88	274	162	112	18.0	15.6	22.6	8.7	6.8	13.5
3	158	86	72	94	46	48	64	40	24	6.1	5.0	8.1	2.9	2.2	4.9
4	121	71	50	74	37	37	47	34	13	4.6	4.1	5.7	2.2	1.8	3.4
5	4	3	1	1	1	0	3	2	1	0.2	0.2	0.1	0.1	0.1	0.1
6	33	15	18	18	8	10	15	7	8	1.3	0.9	2.0	0.6	0.4	1.2
7	1383	1000	383	560	311	249	823	689	134	53.1	58.1	43.3	25.6	25.5	25.9
8	189	119	70	114	67	47	75	52	23	7.3	6.9	7.9	3.5	3.0	4.7
9	111	85	26	41	26	15	70	59	11	4.3	4.9	2.9	2.1	2.2	1.8
10	152	89	63	87	50	37	65	39	26	5.8	5.2	7.1	2.8	2.3	4.3
11	1	1	0	0	0	0	1	0	1	0.0	0.0	0.1	0.0	0.0	0.1
12	0	0	0	0	0	0	0	0	0	0.0	0.0	0.0	0.0	0.0	0.0
13	0	0	0	0	0	0	0	0	0	0.0	0.0	0.0	0.0	0.0	0.0
14	260	146	114	118	66	52	142	80	62	10.0	8.5	12.9	4.8	3.7	7.7
15	133	76	57	62	36	26	71	40	31	5.1	4.4	6.4	2.5	1.9	3.9
16	981	713	268	414	255	159	567	458	109	37.6	41.4	30.3	18.2	18.2	18.1
17	809	709	100	232	192	40	577	517	60	31.0	41.2	11.3	15.0	18.1	6.8
18	552	511	41	134	115	19	418	396	22	21.2	29.7	4.6	10.2	13.0	2.8
المجموع Total	5396	3916	1480	2158	1326	832	3238	2590	648	207.1	227.4	167.4	100.0	100.0	100.0
حجم السكان Population Size II	2606000	1722000	884000							100000	100000	100000	100000	100000	

I Causes of death given in annex 1
II World Population Prospects - The 2000 Revision.

أسباب الوفيات في الملحق رقم 1 I
آفاق سكان العالم – مراجعة عام 2000. II

ملحق رقم 1 : التصنيف الدولي لأسباب الوفاة

Annex 1: International Classification of Causes of Death

Serial no.	Cause of Death	سبب الوفاة	رقم مسلسل
1	Certain infectious and parasitic diseases	امراض معدية وطفيلية معينة	1
2	Neoplasms	الأورام	2
3	Endocrine, nutritional and metabolic dseases	امراض الغدد الصماء والتغذية والتمثيل الغذائي	3
4	Disorders of the blood and blood-forming organs and certain disorders involving the immune mechanism	اضطرابات معينة تشمل اضطرابات الدم واعضاء تكوين الدم واضطرابات الإضطرابات العقلية والسلوكية المناعة	4
5	Mental and behavioural disorders	الإضطرابات العقلية والسلوكية	5
6	Diseases of the nervous system	امراض الجهاز العصبي واعضاء الحس	6
7	Diseases of the circulatory system	امراض الجهاز الدوري الدموي	7
8	Diseases of the respiratory system	امراض الجهاز التنفسي	8
9	Diseases of the digestive system	امراض الجهاز الهضمي	9
10	Diseases of the genitourinary system	امراض الجهاز التناسلي البولي	10
11	Pregnancy, child birth and the puerperium	مضاعفات الحمل والولادة والنفاس	11
12	Diseases of the skin and subcutaneous tissue	امراض الجلد والنسيج تحت الجلد	12
13	Diseases of the musculoskeletal system and connective tissue	امراض الجهاز الهيكلي العظمي والنسيج الضام	13
14	Congenital malformations, deformations and chromosomal abnormalities	تشوهات خلقية وعاهات وشذوذ كروموزمي	14
15	Certain conditions originating in the perinental period	اسباب معينة لحالات المرضى والوفاة حول موعد الولادة	15
16	Symptoms, signs and abnormal clinical and laboratory findings, not elsewhere classified	امراض وحالات غير معينة وغير مشخصة في مكان اخر	16
17	Injury, poisoning and certain other consequences of external causes	الإصابات والتسمم ونتائج اخرى معينة لأسباب خارجية	17
18	Codes for special purposes	حالات غير مشخصة	18
19	Diseases of the eye and adnexa	امراض النظر	19
20	Diseases of the ear and mastoid process	امراض السمع	20
21	External causes of morbidity and mortality	لأسباب خارجية للمرضى والوفاة	21
22	Factors influencing health status and contact with health services	عوامل تؤثر على الوضع الصحي والاتصال بالخدمات الصحية	22

القسم الثالث
Section Three

الزواج والطلاق
Marriages and Divorces

بناء على البيانات الوطنية عن الزواج والطلاق.

[3] أن المعدلات المعروضة في هذا القسم حسبت بناء على البيانات الوطنية عن الزواج والطلاق.

يعرض القسم الثالث من هذا التقرير: "المتزوجين الزواج والطلاق"، بيانات عن متوسط العمر عند الزواج الأول، والمعدلات العام للزواج والطلاق في منطقة الإسكوا منذ عام 2000 وحتى آخر سنة تتوافر فيها البيانات عن كل بلد[3]. ويحتوي هذا القسم على جدولين مع الأشكال البيانية الخاصة بها.

(أ) الجدول 17، يعرض بيانات عن متوسط العمر عند الزواج الأول حسب الجنسية والجنس؛

وتشير بيانات عام 2005 إلى أن الأردن سجلت أعلى متوسط عمر عند الزواج الأول (24.7) و 26.8 للنساء) ووسجلت فلسطين أدنى متوسط عمر عند الزواج الأول (24.7) للذكور و 19.4 سنة للنساء، كذلك تبين البيانات اختلاف بين البلدان في متوسط عمر الزواج الأول أعلى منه للمواطنين وغير المواطنين: أن متوسط عمر غير المواطنين عند الزواج الأول أعلى منه للمواطنين: مثلا في البحرين (27.7) سنة للرجل غير البحريني و 26.2 سنة للرجل البحريني؛ 24.3 سنة للمرأة غير البحرينية و 22.5 سنة للمرأة البحرينية؛ وفي قطر 28.9 سنة للرجل غير القطري و 26.4 سنة للرجل القطري؛ و 25.6 سنة للمرأة غير القطرية و 23.8 سنة للمرأة القطرية.

(ب) الجدول 18، يعرض بيانات عن معدلات الزواج والطلاق الخام؛

في عام 2005، كان أعلى معدل خام للزواج لكل ألف من السكان في سوريا (4.3) والسعودية (4.3) والكويت (4.6) بينما سجلت قطر (3.4)، والسعودية (4.3) والكويت (4.6) أدنى معدلات خام للزواج لكل ألف من السكان. ومن جهة ثانية، بلغ معدل خام للزواج في كل من قطر ومصر (0.8 و 0.9) أدنى من ألف من السكان. وقد وصلت أدنى معدل خام للزواج في كل من الأردن (1.8) يليه الكويت (1.7) لكل ألف من السكان. بينما كان أعلاه في الأردن (9.9) وليبان (9.5) لكل ألف من السكان.

Section III of this Bulletin, entitled "Marriage and Divorce", presents data on crude rates of marriage and divorce in the ESCWA region from 2000 to the most recent year for which data is available for each country[3]. This section contains two tables and their respective graphs.

(a) Table 17, presents mean age at first marriage by nationality and sex

The data indicate that in 2005, the highest mean age at first marriage was in Jordan (29.7 years for the men and 26.8 years for the women) and lowest mean age at first marriage was in Palestine (24.7 years for the men and 19.4 years for the women) Moreover, data showed a variation among the countries in the national and non-national's mean age of marriage. Non-national got married later than the national such as in Bahrain (27.7 years for the non Bahraini man against 26.2 years for the Bahraini man) (24.3 years for the non Bahraini woman against 22.5 years for the Bahraini woman) similarly in Qatar (28.9 years for the non Qatari man against 26.4 years for the Qatari man) (25.6 years for the non Qatari woman against 23.8 years for the Qatari woman)

(b) Table 18, presents data on marriage and divorce crude rates;

In 2005, the highest crude marriage rates per thousand population were in Syria (10.1) followed by Jordan (9.9) and Lebanon (9.5). While Qatar (3.4), Saudi Arabia (4.3) and Kuwait (4.6) ranked the lowest crude marriage rates per thousand population. From the other side, crude divorce rates were higher in Jordan (1.8) followed by Kuwait (1.7) per 1000 population while Qatar and Egypt scored the lowest crude marriage rates per thousand population (0.8 and 0.9 respectively).

[3] The rates presented in this section have been calculated on the basis of national figures for the number of marriages and divorces.

جدول 17 : متوسط العمر عند الزواج الأول حسب الجنسية والجنس

Table 17 : Mean Age at First Marriage by nationality and sex

Country/ Year	TOTAL المجموع		Nationals المواطنون		Non Nationals غير مواطنين		البلد / السنة
	رجال Men	نساء Women	رجال Men	نساء Women	رجال Men	نساء Women	
BAHRAIN							**البحرين**
2005	26.5	22.7	26.2	22.5	27.7	24.3	2005
2004	26.5	22.8	26.2	22.5	28.2	24.9	2004
2003	26.6	22.7	26.5	22.5	27.2	24.8	2003
2002	26.6	22.8	26.4	22.4	30.8	25.9	2002
2001	26.6	22.9	26.5	22.5	28.0	25.8	2001
2000	26.3	25.0	26.2	22.3	27.8	25.4	2000
EGYPT							**مصر**
2005	28.8	23.2	:	:	:	:	2005
2004	28.6	22.1	:	:	:	:	2004
2003	29.0	23.1	:	:	:	:	2003
2002	29.2	23.1	:	:	:	:	2002
2001	28.7	25.5	:	:	:	:	2001
2000	28.6	25.3	:	:	:	:	2000
JORDAN							**الأردن**
2005	29.7	26.8	:	:	:	:	2005
2004	29.3	25.9	:	:	:	:	2004
2003	29.8	27.2	:	:	:	:	2003
2002	29.3	26.8	:	:	:	:	2002
2001	29.3	26.6	:	:	:	:	2001
2000	28.9	25.8	:	:	:	:	2000

جدول 17 (تابع): متوسط العمر عند الزواج الأول حسب الجنسية والجنس

Table 17 (cont'd): Mean Age at First Marriage by nationality and sex

Country/Year	TOTAL المجموع		Nationals المواطنون		Non Nationals غير مواطنين		السنة / البلد
	رجال Men	نساء Women	رجال Men	نساء Women	رجال Men	نساء Women	
OMAN							**عمان**
2004	...	...	...	...	...	...	2004
2003	...	...	...	...	...	...	2003
2002	...	...	...	...	...	...	2002
2001	...	...	...	...	...	...	2001
2003	...	...	28.0	25.0	...	...	2003
2000	...	...	26.4	23.5	...	...	2000
PALESTINE							**فلسطين**
2006	24.7	19.5	...	...	...	...	2006
2005	24.7	19.4	...	...	...	...	2005
2004	24.6	19.3	...	...	...	...	2004
2003	24.6	19.4	...	...	...	...	2003
2002	24.2	19.0	...	...	...	...	2002
2001	24.2	19.0	...	...	...	...	2001
2000	24.1	18.9	...	...	...	...	2000
QATAR							**قطر**
2006	27.7	24.6	26.4	23.6	28.9	25.6	2006
2005	27.8	24.5	26.7	23.9	28.8	25.1	2005
2004	29.1	24.7	29.2	24.8	28.9	24.5	2004
2003	28.4	24.3	27.3	24.1	29.4	24.4	2003
2002	28.0	25.5	27.1	23.8	28.9	24.9	2002
2001	27.9	24.5	27.0	23.8	28.8	25.1	2001
2000	27.9	24.3	27.1	23.8	28.7	24.7	2000

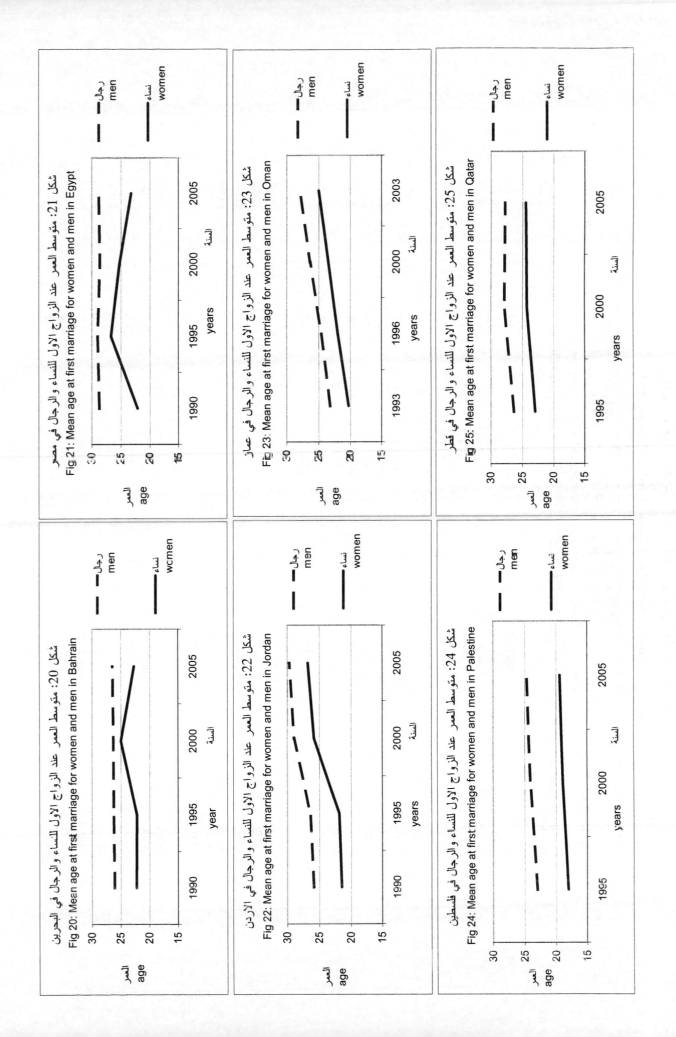

شكل 21: متوسط العمر عند الزواج الأول للنساء والرجال في مصر
Fig 21: Mean age at first marriage for women and men in Egypt

شكل 23: متوسط العمر عند الزواج الأول للنساء والرجال في عمان
Fig 23: Mean age at first marriage for women and men in Oman

شكل 25: متوسط العمر عند الزواج الأول للنساء والرجال في قطر
Fig 25: Mean age at first marriage for women and men in Qatar

شكل 20: متوسط العمر عند الزواج الأول للنساء والرجال في البحرين
Fig 20: Mean age at first marriage for women and men in Bahrain

شكل 22: متوسط العمر عند الزواج الأول للنساء والرجال في الأردن
Fig 22: Mean age at first marriage for women and men in Jordan

شكل 24: متوسط العمر عند الزواج الأول للنساء والرجال في فلسطين
Fig 24: Mean age at first marriage for women and men in Palestine

جدول رقم : 18 معدلات (أ، ب، ج، د) الزواج والطلاق الخام منذ عام 2000

Table 18 : Marriage and Divorce Crude Rates[(a, b, c, d)] since 2000

COUNTRY/ YEAR	حالات الزواج Number of Marriages	معدل الزواج الخام (لكل) من السكان Crude Marriage Rates (per 1000 population)	حالات الطلاق Number of Divorces	معدل الطلاق الخام (لكل) من السكان 1000 Crude Divorce Rates (per 1000 population)	السنة / البلد
BAHRAIN					البحرين
2005	4669	6.4	1051	1.4	2005
2004	4667	6.5	1031	1.4	2004
2003	5373	7.4	923	1.3	2003
2002	4909	6.9	838	1.2	2002
2001	4504	6.9	801	1.2	2001
2000	3963	6.2	769	1.2	2000
EGYPT					مصر
2006	505453	6.8	63158	0.9	2006
2005	522751	7.1	65047	0.9	2005
2004	550709	7.6	64496	0.9	2004
2003	537092	7.5	69867	1.0	2003
2002	510517	7.2	70069	1.0	2002
2001	457534	6.6	70279	1.0	2001
2000	592381	8.7	68991	1.0	2000
IRAQ					العراق
2004	262554	9.4	...	...	2004
2003	256494	10.2	...	...	2003
2002	...	...	...	...	2002
2001	...	...	...	...	2001
2000	171134	7.5	...	...	2000
JORDAN					الأردن
2006	59335	10.4	11413	2.0	2006
2005	56418	9.9	10231	1.8	2005
2004	53754	9.7	9791	1.8	2004
2003	48784	8.9	9022	1.6	2003
2002	46873	8.8	9032	1.7	2002
2001	49794	9.9	9017	1.8	2001
2000	45608	9.3	8241	1.7	2000

جدول رقم 18 (تابع): معدلات الزواج والطلاق الخام منذ عام 2000

Table 18 (cont'd): Marriage and Divorce Crude Rates[1] (a, b, c, d) since 2000

COUNTRY/ YEAR	Number of Marriages	Crude Marriage Rates (per 1000 population)	Number of Divorces	Crude Divorce Rates (per 1000 population)	السنة
KUWAIT					**الكويت**
2005	12419	4.6	4538	1.7	2005
2004	12359	4.7	4899	1.9	2004
2003	12246	4.9	3998	1.6	2003
2002	11973	4.9	3891	1.6	2002
2001	11830	6.0	3851	2.0	2001
2000	10785	5.6	3649	1.9	2000
LEBANON					**لبنان**
2006	32576	8.0	4819	1.2	2006
2005	33837	9.5	5266	1.5	2005
2004	33644	9.5	4311	1.4	2004
2003	35841	9.8	4793	1.3	2003
2002	35392	9.8	4536	1.3	2002
2001	33704	10.0	4617	1.4	2001
2000	32586	9.3	4220	1.2	2000
PALESTINE					**فلسطين**
2006	28233	7.2	3756	1.0	2006
2005	28876	7.8	4211	1.1	2005
2004	27634	7.7	3961	1.1	2004
2003	26267	7.4	3909	1.1	2003
2002	22611	6.6	3046	0.9	2002
2001	24635	7.4	3687	1.1	2001
2000	23890	7.5	3546	1.1	2000

البلد / السنة — حالات الزواج — معدل الزواج الخام (لكل 1000 من السكان) — حالات الطلاق — معدل الطلاق الخام (لكل 1000 من السكان)

جدول رقم 18 (تابع) : معدلات (أ، ب، ج، د) الزواج والطلاق الخام منذ عام 2000

Table 18 (cont'd): Marriage and Divorce Crude Rates[1] (a, b, c, d) since 2000

COUNTRY/ YEAR	حالات الزواج Number of Marriages	معدل الزواج الخام (لكل) 1000 من السكان Crude Marriage Rates (per 1000 population)	حالات الطلاق Number of Divorces	معدل الطلاق الخام (لكل) 1000 من السكان Crude Divorce Rates (per 1000 population)	البلد / السنة السنة
QATAR					**قطر**
2006	3019	3.7	826	1.0	2006
2005	2734	3.4	643	0.8	2005
2004	2649	3.4	787	1.0	2004
2003	2550	4.2	790	1.3	2003
2002	2351	3.9	732	1.2	2002
2001	2194	3.8	566	1.0	2001
2000	2096	3.7	615	1.1	2000
KINGDOM OF SAUDI ARABIA					**المملكة العربية السعودية**
2006	119294	4.9	24862	1.0	2006
2005	105066	4.3	24318	1.0	2005
2004	111063	4.6	24435	1.0	2004
2003	98343	4.1	20794	0.9	2003
2002	90982	3.9	18765	0.8	2002
2001	81576	3.9	16725	0.8	2001
2000	79595	3.9	18583	0.9	2000
SYRIAN ARAB REPUBLIC [II, III]					**الجمهورية العربية السورية** [II, III]
2006	205557	...	19984	...	2006
2005	179075	10.1	17821	1.0	2005
2004	178166	10.3	17336	1.0	2004
2003	204944	12.0	15134	0.9	2003
2002	174449	10.4	14314	0.9	2002
2001	153842	9.4	13077	0.8	2001
2000	139843	8.8	11863	0.7	2000

[II] Includes Syrian Nationals only   [II] تشمل المواطنين السوريين فقط

[III] Population Estimates: national sources (after adjustment)   [III] تقديرات السكان: مصادر وطنية (من بعد التعديل)

-82-

جدول رقم 18 (تابع): معدلات الزواج والطلاق الخام منذ عام 2000

Table 18 (cont'd): Marriage and Divorce Crude Rates[1(a, b, c, d)] since 2000

COUNTRY/ YEAR البلد / السنة	Number of Marriages حالات الزواج	Crude Marriage Rates (per 1000 population) معدل الزواج الخام (لكل الخام) من السكان 1000	Number of Divorces حالات الطلاق	Crude Divorce Rates (per 1000 population) معدل الطلاق الخام (لكل) من السكان 1000
UNITED ARAB EMIRATES الإمارات العربية المتحدة				
2005	12751	2.8	3364	0.7
2004	12794	3.0	3577	0.8
2003	12277	4.1	3243	1.1
2002	11285	3.8	3390	1.2
2001	10030	3.8	2832	1.1
2000	8970	3.4	2392	0.9
YEMEN اليمن				
2004	715	0.0	33	0.0
2003	600	0.0	104	0.0
2002	10934	0.6	998	0.1
2001	9120	0.5	617	0.0
2000	5375	0.3	507	0.0

[1-a] Population estimates for 2000 and 2001 taken from World Population Prospects: 2000 Revision تقدير ات السكان لعامي 2000 و 2001 مستمدة من آفاق سكان العالم: مراجعة 2000

[1-b] Population estimates for 2002 and 2003 taken from World Population Prospects: 2002 Revision تقديرات سكان عام 2002 و 2003 مستمدة من آفاق سكان العالم: مراجعة 2002

[1-c] Population estimates for 2004 and 2005 taken from World Population Prospects: 2004 Revision تقديرات سكان عام 2004 و 2005 مستمدة من آفاق سكان العالم: مراجعة 2004

[1-d] Population estimates for 2006 taken from World Population Prospects: 2006 Revision تقدير ات سكان عام 2006 مستمدة من آفاق سكان العالم: مراجعة 2006

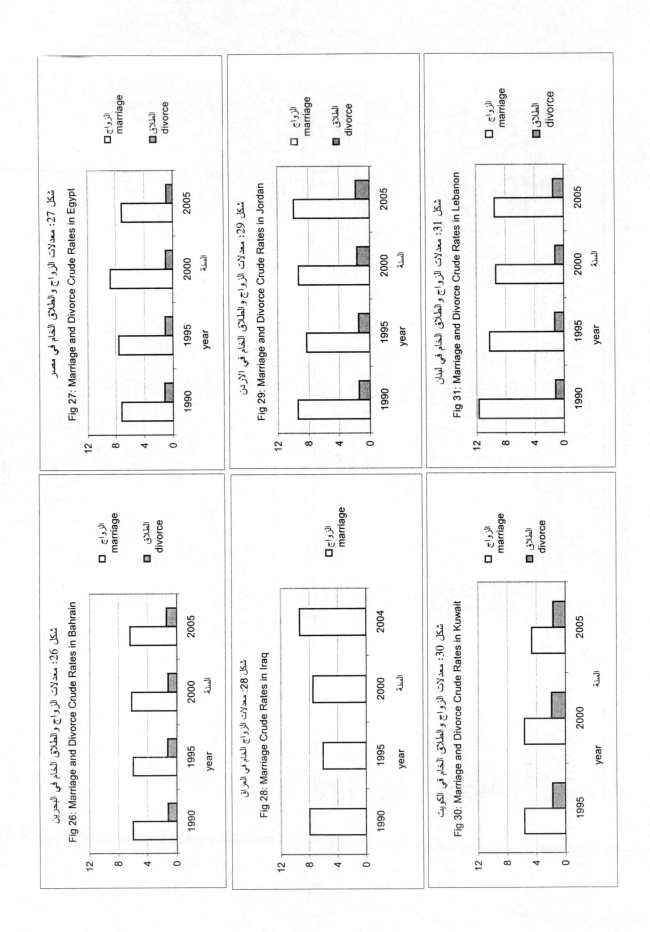

شكل 26: معدلات الزواج والطلاق الخام في البحرين
Fig 26: Marriage and Divorce Crude Rates in Bahrain

شكل 27: معدلات الزواج والطلاق الخام في مصر
Fig 27: Marriage and Divorce Crude Rates in Egypt

شكل 28: معدلات الزواج الخام في العراق
Fig 28: Marriage Crude Rates in Iraq

شكل 29: معدلات الزواج والطلاق الخام في الأردن
Fig 29: Marriage and Divorce Crude Rates in Jordan

شكل 30: معدلات الزواج والطلاق الخام في الكويت
Fig 30: Marriage and Divorce Crude Rates in Kuwait

شكل 31: معدلات الزواج والطلاق الخام في لبنان
Fig 31: Marriage and Divorce Crude Rates in Lebanon

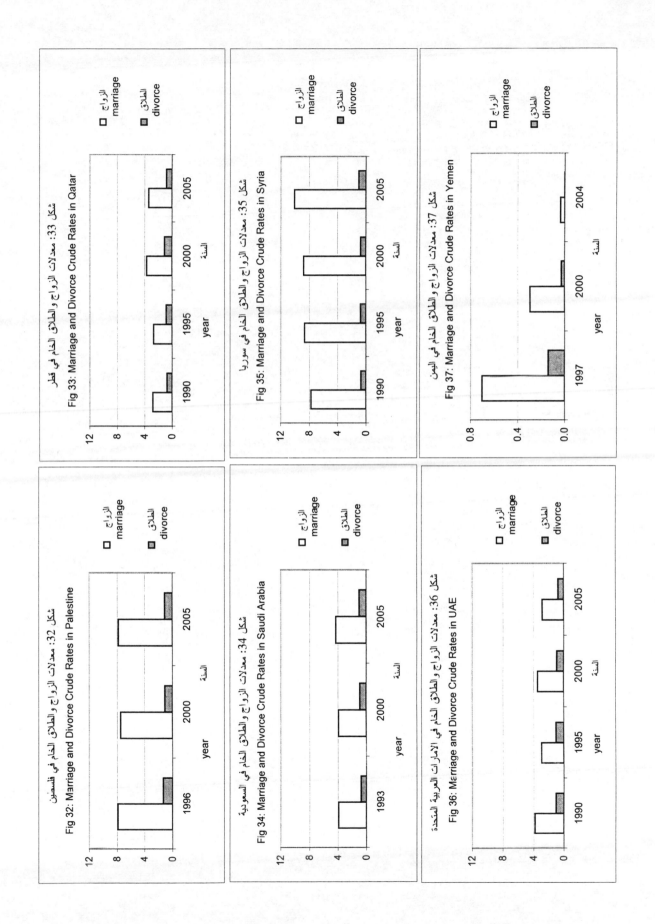

شكل 32: معدلات الزواج والطلاق الخام في فلسطين
Fig 32: Marriage and Divorce Crude Rates in Palestine

شكل 33: معدلات الزواج والطلاق الخام في قطر
Fig 33: Marriage and Divorce Crude Rates in Qatar

شكل 34: معدلات الزواج والطلاق الخام في السعودية
Fig 34: Marriage and Divorce Crude Rates in Saudi Arabia

شكل 35: معدلات الزواج والطلاق الخام في سوريا
Fig 35: Marriage and Divorce Crude Rates in Syria

شكل 36: معدلات الزواج والطلاق الخام في الإمارات العربية المتحدة
Fig 36: Marriage and Divorce Crude Rates in UAE

شكل 37: معدلات الزواج والطلاق الخام في اليمن
Fig 37: Marriage and Divorce Crude Rates in Yemen

SOURCES:

Egypt

1. Central Agency for Public Mobilization and Statistics (CAPMAS). 2002. The Statistical Yearbook 1994-2001. Cairo.

2. Central Agency for Public Mobilization and Statistics (CAPMAS). 2000. The Statistical Yearbook 1993-1999. Cairo.

Iraq

1. Central Statistical Organization. 2006. Annual Abstract of Statistics 2005/2006. Baghdad.

2. Central Statistical Organization. 2004. Annual Abstract of Statistics 2004. Baghdad.

3. Central Statistical Organization. 2003 Annual Abstract of Statistics 2003. Baghdad.

4. Central Statistical Organization. 2002 Annual Abstract of Statistics 2002. Baghdad.

5. Central Statistical Organization. 2001 Annual Abstract of Statistics 2001. Baghdad.

Jordan

1. Department of Statistics. 2003. Statistical Yearbook 2000. No. 53. Amman.

Kuwait

1. Ministry of Planning. 2005. Annual Bulletin for Vital Statistics - Births and Deaths 1996. Kuwait

Oman

1. Ministry of Health. Directorate General of Planning. 2002. Annual Health Report 2001 A.D. 1421 A.H. Muscat

المصادر :

مصر

1- الجهاز المركزي للتعبئة العامة والإحصاء. 2002. الكتاب الإحصائي السنوي 1994-2001. القاهرة.

2- الجهاز المركزي للتعبئة العامة والإحصاء. 2000. الكتاب الإحصائي السنوي 1993-1999. القاهرة.

العراق

1- الجهاز المركزي للإحصاء. 2006. المجموعة الإحصائية السنوية 2005/2006. بغداد.

2- الجهاز المركزي للإحصاء. 2004. المجموعة الإحصائية السنوية 2004. بغداد.

3- الجهاز المركزي للإحصاء. 2003. المجموعة الإحصائية السنوية 2003. بغداد.

4- الجهاز المركزي للإحصاء. 2002. المجموعة الإحصائية السنوية 2002. بغداد.

5- الجهاز المركزي للإحصاء. 2001. المجموعة الإحصائية السنوية 2001. بغداد.

الأردن

1- دائرة الإحصاءات العامة. 2003. الكتاب الإحصائي السنوي 2002. العدد 53. عمان.

الكويت

1- وزارة التخطيط. 2005. النشرة السنوية للإحصاءات الحيوية – المواليد والوفيات. 2005

عمان

1- وزارة الصحة. المديرية العامة للتخطيط. 2002. التقرير الصحي السنوي عام 2001. مسقط 1421هـ.

Syrian Arab Republic

1. Central Bureau of Statistics. 2003. Statistical Abstract 2003. Fifty six year. Damascus.

2. Central Bureau of Statistics. 2002. Statistical Abstract 2002. Fifty five year. Damascus.

3. Central Bureau of Statistics. 2000. Statistical Abstract 2000. Fifty three year. Damascus.

United Arab Emirates

1. Central Statistical Department. 2002. Annual Statistical Abstract 2002. Abu Dhabi.

Republic of Yemen

1. Central Statistical Organization. 2002. Statistical Yearbook 2001. Sana'a.

2. Central Statistical Organization. 2001. Statistical Yearbook 2000. Sana'a.

الجمهورية العربية السورية

1– المكتب المركزي للإحصاء. 2003. المجموعة الإحصائية لعام 2003. السنة السادس والخمسون. دمشق.

2– المكتب المركزي للإحصاء. 2002. المجموعة الإحصائية لعام 2002. السنة الخامس والخمسون. دمشق.

3– المكتب المركزي للإحصاء. 2000. المجموعة الإحصائية لعام 2000. السنة الثالثة والخمسون. دمشق.

الإمارات العربية المتحدة

1– الإدارة المركزية للإحصاء. 2002. المجموعة الإحصائية السنوية 2002. أبو ظبي.

الجمهورية اليمنية

1– الجهاز المركزي للإحصاء. 2002. كتاب الإحصاء السنوي 2001. صنعاء.

2– الجهاز المركزي للإحصاء. 2001. كتاب الإحصاء السنوي 2000. صنعاء.